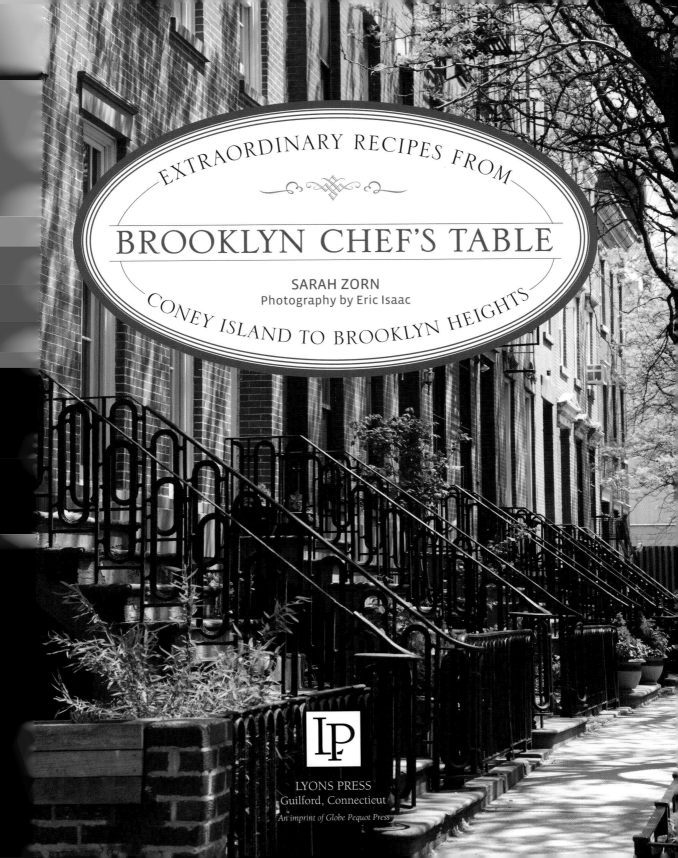

EXTRAORDINARY RECIPES FROM

# BROOKLYN CHEF'S TABLE

SARAH ZORN
Photography by Eric Isaac

CONEY ISLAND TO BROOKLYN HEIGHTS

LYONS PRESS
Guilford, Connecticut
An imprint of Globe Pequot Press

Restaurants and chefs often come and go, and menus are ever-changing.
We recommend you call ahead to obtain current information before
visiting any of the establishments in this book.

To buy books in quantity for corporate use
or incentives, call **(800) 962-0973**
or e-mail **premiums@GlobePequot.com.**

All photography by Eric Isaac

Editor: Amy Lyons
Project Editor: Lynn Zelem
Text Design: Libby Kingsbury
Layout Artist: Nancy Freeborn

Library of Congress Cataloging-in-Publication Data is available on file.

ISBN 978-0-7627-8635-0

Printed in the United States of America

10 9 8 7 6 5 4 3 2 1

No matter what my bank account says, I'm rich beyond measure because of my husband, Fred, my mother, Risa, my grandmother, Cecil, my brother, Josh, and my sweetheart, Rowdy. I love and appreciate you all so much more than words can ever express.

# CONTENTS

# Acknowledgments

First of all, many thanks to Amy Lyons, who contacted me out of the blue one day and, amazingly, asked if I wanted to author a cookbook about restaurants in Brooklyn. Um, yes please. Thank you, Eric Isaac, for being just as passionate about this project as I am, and for taking such glorious photos (because even I am guilty of cracking open cookbooks just for the pretty pictures inside). And thanks to Fernando Souto and Anderson Zaca for being such a help and making us laugh during all those days on set. Bet the food was a lot better than it is at fashion shoots, eh, fellas? Thanks to my fantastic agent at Folio, Melissa Sarver, for taking care of business, and connecting me with Jordan Hall, who tirelessly transcribed hours of audio so I could really get down to writing. Much appreciation to Sharon Kuntz, our tireless publicist at Globe Pequot, for helping bring our beloved *Brooklyn Chef's Table* into the public consciousness. And of course, endless thanks to all of the amazing restaurants that generously (and under deadline!) handed over their recipes and submitted to various photo shoots and interviews. You are my culinary idols, and it's been an honor to share your stories between the covers of this book!

My everlasting appreciation to Staci White and Ronnie Cohen, who always knew where my heart belonged, and selflessly supported me so I could get to where I needed to be. To Pamela Mitchell, a class act who gave me my first big break, taking me under her wing at *Every Day with Rachael Ray*. And thank you, Gersh Kuntzman, for helping me find my sweet spot, and starting the ball rolling by making me your "Foodie-in-Chief" at the *Brooklyn Paper*. I learned so very much from you, usually via humorous tirades over e-mail. I'm forever grateful to have been given the chance to continue to write about food and Brooklyn for the brilliant *Brooklyn Magazine*—Mike Conklin and Daniel Stedman, you are probably two of the coolest guys to work for, ever. But as much as I adore Brooklyn, a thousand thank yous to the fabulous Danyelle Freeman, for taking me in at Restaurant Girl and helping me see that some pretty cool stuff happens on the other side of the bridge too.

Lots of love to my brilliant twin brother, Josh, who patiently put up with all of my food shenanigans from an early age. Thank you for being complicit in my kitchen experiments (like "Spice Rack Home Fries" and anything that could be made from Bisquick mix!). And thank you for gamely leaving restaurants twenty minutes after sitting down, because I decided I didn't like anything on the menu. I was a real creep.

OK, here's the crying onto my computer part. The only downside to writing this book is that my beloved grandma, Cecil Novikoff, isn't around to see it. The ways in which you helped shape and better my life, Grandma (especially as it pertains to food), could form the basis of an entire novel. I remember lying on my stomach by your rocking chair and poring through your collection of cookbooks, over and over again. Who would have guessed that one day, I'd write something that could have potentially shared shelf space with *The Silver Palate Cookbook* and *The Joy of Cooking*? I wish I could have shared this moment with you.

I don't even know where to start when it comes to my mother, Risa Novikoff. For all intents and purposes, you gave over your life for me, so I could make mine into anything I wanted. And even though that eventually led me to a career in writing, I'll always come up empty when I try to find the right words. It can't be expressed, either in two lines or two thousand, the endless love and appreciation I have for you, your boundless strength, and your perpetual support.

And lastly, to the two great loves of my life. Fred Zorn, I never allowed myself to believe that you were out there, and I can't imagine one day, one moment, one breath without you. You are husband, home, best friend, and confidant all wrapped into one, and inspire me to be a better person every day. I love you fully and eternally. And to my sweet, darling Rowdy, the best little guy anyone could ask for, who fills my heart and puts a smile on my face every single day. Now that the book is done, Mama will finally take a break from tapping on that damn screen.

# Introduction

As a kid growing up in the 1980s in Brooklyn, I had already begun to chart my borough, indeed, my life, by what I ate, and where, and when. Summer was all about trips to Nathan's on Coney Island with my mother and twin brother, sitting on the boardwalk, spearing fat, salty fries with little red pitchforks, and trying to shield our snappy-skinned hot dogs from swirling clouds of sand and the seagulls that swooped overhead. When the weather turned cool we moved a little further inland to Brighton Beach, for pillowy cushions of potato from Mrs. Stahl's Knishes. While sweet versions in blueberry, apple, or farmer cheese and cherry may have seemed a more obvious order for a ten-year-old girl, I was much more likely to request broccoli, cabbage, or mushroom—to the clucking approval of a throng of assembled Russian ladies in babushkas.

Wintertime meant dinner at throwback red-sauce palaces like Colandrea New Corner or Monte's Venetian Room, where everything was ordered by the platterful in

various permutations of "Francese," "Parmigiana," or "Fra Diavolo." And if we were really feeling adventurous, we'd take the subway downtown for cheesecake at Junior's, or to Brooklyn Heights for Polish food at Theresa's, or maybe even follow the promenade all the way out to DUMBO for pizza at Grimaldi's. Of course, we never even thought about frequenting Red Hook, Bed Stuy, or Park Slope west of Sixth Avenue. What single mother with two young children would, in those days? And Williamsburg, Greenpoint, and Bushwick were completely off of our radar—unmitigated dead zones when it came to dining out. Oh, how times have changed.

Although Brooklyn remained the center of my food world, I began to notice, as I got older, how hard it was to convince friends and colleagues to venture across the bridge to eat with me. Or how many restaurant critics staunchly refused to admit we even existed. Except for one, Robert Sietsema, whose regular *Village Voice* column I took to reading like the gospels. I was swept away as he described tiny taco stands tucked in back of grimy bodegas in Sunset Park, or impossibly exotic West Indian restaurants, frequented by Pakistani cabdrivers in Flatbush, in adulating terms usually reserved for white-tablecloth restaurants on the Upper East Side.

And then came The Great Brooklyn Restaurant Boom. The groundswell began quietly at the tail end of the '90s, at places like al di là in Park Slope, where husband and wife team Anna Klinger and Emiliano Coppa set out to redefine authentic Italian food (and ushered in

the no-reservations policy and resulting hour and a half–long wait times.) It continued along to Cobble Hill at Saul, where chef and owner Saul Bolton made the borough a contender on the fine-dining scene, eventually bringing our own Michelin star to Smith Street. Brooklyn's restaurant momentum caught fire in earnest in Williamsburg, Greenpoint, and Bushwick, where young, classically trained chefs began to flee the lines in stuffy, Manhattan kitchens, taking advantage of outer-borough rents and eager, locally minded clientele, opening their own intimate eateries with exposed-brick walls, reclaimed-wood tables, market-inspired menus, and wallet-friendly prices. And those plucky food artisans who still couldn't afford a brick-and-mortar? They started a fleet of mobile eateries, beginning with the cluster of food trucks at the Red Hook Ballfields, starring the Vendy Award–winning Solber Pupusas. They invested in edible timeshares, or pop-ups, opening for a few nights at a time at existing restaurants, reducing overhead and creating the kind of buzz that money could never buy. And they opened makeshift stands at Brooklyn Flea in 2008, and at Smorgasburg, its food-dedicated offshoot, in 2011, a weekend event so popular, it eventually expanded to that other far-flung borough, Manhattan.

And now, finally, it's become less of a trend to talk about how trendy the Brooklyn dining scene is, and just an accepted fact. That from Crown Heights to Mill Basin, Prospect Heights to Bensonhurst, we're home to some of the best and most varied and most destination-worthy restaurants, not just in NYC, but throughout the entire country. So when you thumb through this book, I hope that you see it as more than just a collection of recipes. I hope that by reading the stories of the members of our restaurant community, the ones who grew up here and never left, or who came from other countries in search of a dream, or merely migrated across the bridge in order to better articulate their craft, you'll see Brooklyn expressed through that glorious medium, food. Brooklyn as it was, Brooklyn as it is, and Brooklyn as it will be, far into the foreseeable future.

# A.L.C Italian Grocery

8613 3rd Avenue, Bay Ridge
(718) 836-3200
ALCITALIANGROCERY.COM
Owner: Louis Coluccio
Chef: Michael Kogan

A.L.C Italian Grocery in Bay Ridge is modeled after old-school *salumerias,* like D. Coluccio and Sons in Bensonhurst. The kind that used to dot the South Brooklyn landscape, serving as gathering points for locals picking up their weekly provisions of air-dried salami. That's because it's run by Louis Coluccio, the son/grandson of those original Coluccios, who manages to retain the spirit of the original—feisty Sicilian grandmothers can haggle over the price of imported extra-virgin olive oil and fat-capped guanciale—while still providing safe haven to local/seasonal fanatics (reliable suppliers include Salvatore BKLYN, Bien Cuit, and Brooklyn Cured). "We're not stuffy or pretentious; we're not looking to re-create anything," Coluccio assures. "We're just taking what we know and love and adding to it, modernizing it."

"For example, our chef, Michael Kogan, has created a line of prepared foods, like meatballs made with Pat LaFrieda beef, and bucatini pie with haricots verts, Asiago cheese, and San Marzano tomatoes," he continues. "It's all about educating the next generation about the importance of good quality ingredients."

A.L.C also represents a reprieve in the steady exodus of mom-and-pop shops in Bay Ridge, which will, with any luck, prove part of a legacy as enduring as that of D. Coluccio and Sons. "Growing up, I was unaware of the impact the place had; I just swept floors, grated cheese, and jumped in wherever I was needed," demurs Coluccio. "It's not until you step out of it, and other people tell you the significance and importance of what your grandfather did, that it hits home. The truth is, D. Coluccio and Sons turned an entire section of Brooklyn into an extended family. And we aim to do the same here."

## Bucatini Pie

### (SERVES 8–10)

¼ cup extra-virgin olive oil (plus extra for tossing with pasta)
1 pound bucatini pasta
¼ pound butter or pancetta fat (plus extra for buttering pan)
2 tablespoons flour
1 cup milk
1 cup half-and-half
1 cup shredded fontina

1 cup shredded provolone
1 cup grated Grana Padano
2 cups diced pancetta
1 cup haricots verts (or green beans)
1 cup diced oven-dried tomatoes
¼ cup chopped mixed Italian herbs, like parsley, basil, and oregano
Salt and pepper to taste

Preheat oven to 375°F and butter a 9 x 12-inch baking dish. Bring a large pot of water to a boil with olive oil and a small palmful of salt. Add the bucatini and bring back to a boil, continue to cook until pasta is 90% done. Strain the pasta through a colander, toss with olive oil, and set aside.

While the pasta is cooking, melt the butter in a large saucepot over medium heat until fully melted. Add the flour and whisk together to make a roux. Cook the butter and flour mixture for about 3 minutes without burning. Add the milk and continue whisking until there are no more clumps of flour, then add the half-and-half and continue whisking until the mixture becomes thick and smooth, about 5–8 minutes. This is called a béchamel. Add half of the cheese and stir. Add the other half and stir again until fully melted.

Place the pancetta in a cold pan and put on the stove over a very low flame. Sauté until the fat is rendered out and the pancetta becomes crispy. Drain on paper towels to remove excess fat. Next, blanch the beans in salted, boiling water for approximately 2 minutes and shock in ice water.

In a large bowl, mix the pasta with some cheese sauce until well coated. Toss in the beans, diced tomatoes, pancetta, and herbs and season with salt and pepper. Pour this mixture into the buttered baking dish and place in the oven until the top gets nice and golden brown, approximately 8–10 minutes.

# D. Coluccio & Sons

If you were to walk down 12th Avenue and 60th Street, where Borough Park blends into Sunset Park and Hasidic Jews give way to thickly settled Chinese, you'd find a tiny—almost forgotten—slice of Bensonhurst. Once considered Brooklyn's own Little Italy, there's very little left to document the era of *salumerias, latticinis* and *pasticcerias,* save for a couple of scattered spots on 13th and 17th Avenues, at least ten streets away. But then you happen upon D. Coluccio and Sons. Opened in 1962 by Calabrian native Domenico Coluccio (and eventually passed down to his two sons), the specialty retail and wholesale shop has since become a haven for a community of Italian expats. Once inside, it's suddenly easy to imagine Brooklyn circa the 1960s, when a rotating stable of regulars wandered in for knobs of fresh mozzarella, beloved products from the Old Country like panettone and torrone, dried beans and pasta, wrinkled, oil-cured olives, and a pound of "your best pro-shoot." Grandson Louis is more than upholding family legacy with A.L.C Grocery in Bay Ridge, but we're counting on even further generations of Coluccios, to keep Italian tradition alive and well in Bensonhurst for many years to come.

# AL DI LÀ TRATTORIA

248 FIFTH AVENUE, PARK SLOPE
(718) 636-8888
ALDILATRATTORIA.COM
CHEF/OWNER: ANNA KLINGER
OWNER: EMILIANO COPPA

You might envision one of the grande dames of Italian cooking in Brooklyn to be some larger-than-life, knife-wielding *nonna,* with a booming voice and an apron half smeared with semolina flour and spaghetti sauce. But the pixie-esque, soft-spoken Anna Klinger looks exactly like what she is—a Park Slope mom—who's just returned from spin class with her son.

And yet her Venetian trattoria, al di là, has consistently been praised as one of the borough's preeminent Italian restaurants. Opened in 1998 on a desolate stretch of Fifth Avenue, it was one of the first Brooklyn eateries to consistently draw in customers from across the bridge, after garnering two stars from Frank Bruni in his review for the *New York Times.* "I don't even know!" Klinger exclaims, when you ask her to theorize on her success. "There just weren't a lot of other restaurant options when we opened. We had

no awning, no siding; we couldn't afford it. Maybe the appeal was that we were in the middle of nowhere, with no name outside, and were hard to find!"

That appeal hasn't even begun to lessen, as anyone who's ever waited up to an hour and a half for a table can readily attest to. "We still get nailed for our no-reservations policy. Whenever people talk about that trend, they talk about us," Klinger laughs. "But it's just that we had no idea how to do it to begin with. My husband, Emiliano, and I were both running the place; it was just me in the kitchen and him out front. And he would be at the door almost in tears because folks were fifteen minutes late, or we were a few minutes late. They'd be shouting at him and it was just a fiasco." Thankfully, it's worth waiting in line for dishes like *malfatti:* pillowy, swiss chard and ricotta gnocchi bathed with brown butter and sage. So how does Klinger achieve such a feather-light consistency? "The drier you can get your greens—whatever greens you use—the lighter they're going to be, because otherwise, you have to add flour. That's truly the trick."

# Malfatti

(SERVES 4–6 AS A LIGHT MAIN COURSE, 6–8 AS A FIRST COURSE)

1 pound ricotta cheese
Kosher salt
4 bunches swiss chard (about 4 pounds)
8 ounces butter
¼ cup flour, plus more for shaping
½ teaspoon freshly grated nutmeg
4 large egg yolks
1 large whole egg
Freshly ground black pepper
24 fresh sage leaves
Parmesan cheese for serving

Drain the ricotta in a sieve lined with cheesecloth overnight in the refrigerator. Measure out 1¼ cups.

Bring a large pot of water, heavily seasoned with salt, to a boil. Trim the chard, removing all stems and large ridges. Add half to the boiling water and cook until soft, about 3 minutes. Fish out and plunge into a bowl of ice water. Repeat with remaining chard.

Squeeze out chard with your hands. On a dish towel, spread the chard in a circle the size of a pie. Roll up the towel and have someone help you twist the ends to squeeze out as much moisture as possible. Pulse in a food processor until fine. Squeeze out in a dish towel once more, until very dry. (You will have about 1 cup.)

Melt half the butter. Mix chard and ricotta. Add melted butter, ¼ cup flour, 1 heaping teaspoon salt and nutmeg and mix again. Drop in egg yolks and egg, season with pepper and stir again. Sprinkle a cutting board with flour. Shape into 1 ounce balls, about 1 tablespoon each, dropping them on the cutting board. You should have 25–30.

Put a teaspoon of flour into a narrow wineglass. Drop in a ball and swirl until it forms an oval. Repeat. (You may need to change the glass.) You may freeze them at this point.

Bring a pot of salted water to a boil. Drop in the malfatti and cook until they float, about 8 minutes. (If frozen, 10 minutes.) Put remaining butter in a small sauté pan and heat until bubbling, shaking the pan. When it smells nutty and turns brown, add sage and cook 30 seconds. Season with salt.

Drain malfatti and place on plates. Spoon on the butter and sage. Grate Parmesan over each plate.

# ALLSWELL

124 BEDFORD AVENUE, WILLIAMSBURG
(347) 799-2743
ALLSWELLNYC.TUMBLR.COM
CHEF/OWNER: NATE SMITH
PASTRY CHEF/OWNER: SOPHIE KAMIN

Nate Smith and Sophie Kamin tend to finish each other's sentences. If he cites his early exposure to food and cooking, she'll interject that his grandmother was a farmer. And if she's sharing tips on making foolproof piecrusts, he'll remind her that she uses a rolling pin to smash down her butter. It's a type of married patter that translates perfectly to their working relationship, he as chef and owner of Allswell, a seasonally minded Williamsburg gastropub, and she as pastry chef, where she provides the ultimate sweet counterpoint to his hearty, savory meals. "She's the opinion and palate I can really rely on and trust like my own," says Smith.

"You understand what the other person is going through in a way you can't when you have separate jobs," adds Kamin. "It generates so much positive energy between us, that working together is mostly positive."

"Yeah, like 99 percent positive," inserts Smith.

In fact, their careers have run parallel for a number of years, from dual stints at Roman's in Fort Greene and Dean Street in Prospect Heights, to a monthly series at Four and Twenty Blackbirds in Gowanus called Pie for Dinner (he began the evenings with rabbit and root vegetables or warm cabbage with wild mushroom pie, and she finished them off with salty nut chess pie with maple cream). "We just kind of took off from there. Everything clicked perfectly for us," says Smith.

"We started dating maybe six or seven months after he moved here," remembers Kamin. "That was probably twelve years ago in Williamsburg. We've been together every moment since."

"Actually," concludes Smith, "we've been for together for thirteen years."

# Guinea Fowl with Baked Navy Beans

(SERVES 4)

Chef's Note: Since Guinea fowl has darker, richer meat than chicken, it's nice to use on special occasions. It's also fun to do higher quality spin-offs of traditional, classic dishes, like baked beans. There's no reason they have to be so, you know, *barbecue*.

*For the beans:*

2 cups dry navy beans

4 cups water

1 cup whole peeled tomatoes

¼ cup sugar

1 tablespoon salt

2 tablespoons vegetable oil

1 cup smoky slab bacon, cut into 1-inch strips, ¼-inch wide

1 Spanish onion, small dice

1 whole clove garlic, chopped fine

1 poblano pepper, small dice

1 tablespoon salt

4 ounces tomato paste

½ cup molasses

½ cup brown sugar

2 tablespoons Dijon mustard

2 tablespoons Worcestershire sauce

½ teaspoon smoked paprika

2 tablespoons red wine vinegar

*For the guinea fowl:*

2 whole guinea fowls

¼ cup vegetable oil

Salt and pepper

1 lemon, cut in half for squeezing

3 tablespoons crème fraîche

3 tablespoons finishing quality extra-virgin olive oil

½ cup finely chopped parsley

To make the beans: Put navy beans into a 2-quart saucepot and top with water. Bring almost to a simmer, being careful not to boil beans. Keep beans at a constant scalding temperature, topping up with water when necessary. Always keep your beans submerged. Beans are done when tender but not broken, about 2–3 hours. When tender, transfer to a bowl and allow to cool completely.

Place tomatoes on a cookie tray lined with a silpat or parchment paper. Season with sugar and salt. Cook until tomatoes have lost about half of their moisture. Tomatoes should begin to get a little color and start to brown. Remove from oven and give a rough chop. Set aside.

In a dutch oven, warm oil until glimmering in pan. Add bacon and cook until golden in color. Add onion, garlic, poblano pepper, and salt. Cook until vegetables are tender.

Add cooked navy beans. Season with tomato paste, molasses, brown sugar, Dijon mustard, Worcestershire sauce, smoked paprika, and vinegar. With a wooden spoon or spatula, make sure all ingredients are well dissolved. Taste for seasoning and adjust if necessary.

This can be done 1 day in advance: Bake in oven set at 325°F for about 2 hours, with lid off, until beans are deep in color and flavor. Be sure to stir often as beans on surface tend to get tough if not rotated. When done, remove from oven and allow to cool to room temperature. Adjust with water to make the beans "saucy"; beans should not be dry.

To make the fowl: Ask your local butcher if they can provide you with a guinea fowl. If not, you can just use chicken. Your butcher may also be able to debone your bird for you, but if you are feeling adventurous, it is simple to do yourself at home (a helpful hint is to look up frenching or deboning a chicken on YouTube for a visual reference). Remove wings from bird by cutting at the wing joint. To halve the bird, begin cutting at the center of the breast, removing the meat from the rib bones, using the rib cavity as a guide. Using your knife, follow all the way down until reaching its back skin, then cut through the skin. The meat from the bird should be completely detached from the rib cavity. Repeat steps on the other side of the bird. To remove leg bone, score along bone on the flesh side of bird, being careful not to puncture through the skin. With bone exposed, carefully remove the bone. Repeat on the other side. You should be left with two boneless half portions.

Preheat oven to 400°F. In a heavy-bottomed pan over high heat, bring oil just to the smoking point. Season bird with salt and pepper on both sides. Gently lay bird skin side down into pan, being careful of splattering oil. Cook just until bird begins to get golden color. At this point, transfer to oven (put pan at bottom of oven on lowest rack). Cook for about 8 minutes or until flesh begins to feel firm. Check skin to make sure it is not getting too much color. If bird begins to take on too much color, move to a higher rack in the oven. When bird is feeling slightly firm, discard hot fat and squeeze lemon over the bird, immediately flipping it to avoid making the skin soggy. Allow bird to rest for 2–3 minutes

To finish: Reheat beans on stovetop until hot, adjusting with water to achieve appropriate saucy consistency, folding in some of the baked tomatoes. Cut fowl by separating leg meat from breast. Following the direction of the wing bone, cut breast into two pieces. Plate beans, place fowl just atop beans, dab plate with a few dollops of crème fraîche, and finish with touches of finishing olive oil. Garnish with parsley.

# MEYER LEMON SHAKER PIE

(MAKES 1 PIE)

Chef's Note: With pie crust, you're trying to coat the flour with fat. So when the fat freezes and then goes in the oven, it melts out and you're left with this pocket of air. That's how you get flakes.

Recipe uses 10-inch removable-bottom tart pan

*For the crust:*

3 cups all-purpose flour

1¼ cups pastry flour

1 teaspoon salt

¼ cup sugar

1 pound butter

Apple cider water (⅓ cup apple cider vinegar
    mixed with 1 cup water and 1 cup ice)

*For the lemon filling:*

10–11 ounces Meyer Lemons
    (about 3-4 lemons depending on size)

2 cups sugar

5 extra large eggs

½ teaspoon salt

*For the crème fraîche ice cream:*

2 cups milk

1 cup sugar

10 egg yolks

4 tablespoons corn syrup

1 quart crème fraîche

To make the dough: Mix all dry ingredients. Cut the butter into long skinny pieces. Loosely mix the butter and flour together. Using a rolling pin, roll the butter into the flour mixture. Scrape the flour and butter using a bench scraper and fold into itself. Repeat with rolling pin. Repeat with scraper. Continue process until the butter and flour are mixed but very dry, with small bits of butter. The dough will look like dry clay in the desert as you are working it together. You will be able to see the layers you are trying to achieve. Add ⅓ cup iced vinegar water, and mix loosely with your fingers to coat the flour and butter with the water. Add another ⅓ cup. Repeat if needed by adding another ¼–⅓ cup of the vinegar water. Use your discretion—the dough should be dry but you should be able to see larger lumps gathering together. Flatten dough out with your hands. Fold on top of itself and press down the dough. Make sure to keep adding in all of the dry crumbs of dough and repeat two more times. Let the dough rest in the fridge for at least 2 hours or freeze until ready to use.

To make the filling: Slice the lemons very thin, preferably using a mandoline. Mix with sugar and let it sit in the fridge overnight. Whisk the eggs and salt until they are blended. Mix the eggs and lemons thoroughly. Make sure the lemons are stored and mixed in a nonreactive container, preferably stainless steel.

To make the ice cream: In a saucepan over medium heat, combine the milk and sugar and bring to almost simmer, until sugar dissolves. Whisk the egg yolks until thick and ribbony (or use an electric mixer). Temper eggs by slowly whisking ½ cup of hot milk into the egg yolks. Slowly add another ½ cup while whisking. Mix the tempered egg yolks into the pot with remaining milk. Cook on low heat until a custard forms,

stirring continuously, roughly 10 minutes. Pass custard through a fine-mesh strainer into a metal container. Put container in an ice bath and let chill. Once chilled, mix custard with crème fraîche. Churn in ice cream mixer according to factory instructions.

To make the pie: Cut the dough in half. Roll out top and bottom on a floured surface to ¼-inch thick. Line pan with bottom crust, leaving 1 inch of excess dough around perimeter. Pour filling into pan. Top with top crust, fold and crimp edges to seal in filling. Cut slits in top crust. Freeze for 30 minutes to an hour. Bake at 350°F until top is very brown and filling is set, about 40–50 minutes. Let sit for 2 hours before serving, to make sure the custard in the filling sets up. Cut into wedges and serve at room temperature with crème fraiche ice cream.

# ANELLA

222 FRANKLIN STREET, GREENPOINT
(718) 389-8102
ANELLABROOKLYN.COM
EXECUTIVE CHEF: TODD ANDREWS
OWNERS: JOSH COHEN AND BLAIR PAPAGNI

You tend to get inspirational responses to the question "what made you decide to become a chef?" Some people were enthralled by reruns of Julia Child on PBS. Others remember sitting in their grandmother's kitchen, watching her make lasagna, arroz con pollo, or chicken soup. Still others were swayed by their first experience eating in a real restaurant, their first taste of a homegrown tomato, or first sniff of a heady summer truffle. "When I was sixteen, I had a friend tell me I could make three more dollars than everyone else if I worked as a cook," Todd Andrews admits sheepishly.

Of course, it didn't take long for him to realize that becoming a chef was more of a passionate pursuit than a moneymaking venture. So when the cooking bug really hit after college, Andrews worked his way up the ranks at multiple restaurants, from hot line to sous chef, and eventually executive chef at Greenpoint's beloved seasonal eatery Anella.

He's actually the perfect fit for the unassuming restaurant, where the humble trappings (bare-bones dining room, cozy backyard, bread baked in terra-cotta

flowerpots) belie thoughtful, masterfully simple food. Particularly delightful are Andrews's handmade cheeses, like milky mozzarella or rich, cream-filled burrata, although unsurprisingly, he's hesitant to take too much credit for either. "When it comes to fresh cheese, it's amazing how little people know about it and how easy it is to make at home," Andrews insists. "But once you've mastered the basics, the possibilities are endless. You can go from mozzarella to burrata to ricotta and even to ricotta salata, which is a little bit more labor intensive. It's just a matter of reading a bit about it and practicing."

## HANDMADE BURRATA CHEESE WITH BASIL SALT & TOMATO JAM

(MAKES 1 ROUND OF CHEESE)

*For the tomato jam:*

15 Roma tomatoes
1 large white onion, finely minced
6 garlic cloves, finely minced
1 cup apple cider vinegar
½ cup sugar
2 star anise
1 tablespoon cayenne
1 cinnamon stick
½ cup olive oil

*For the burrata:*

6 ounces fresh mozzarella curd (can be purchased online or from a specialty cheese shop, like Bedford Cheese Shop or The Garden)
1 cup cream
Salt and pepper
Olive oil

*For the basil salt:*

8–10 large leaves of fresh basil
1 cup sea salt

To make the jam: Using a sharp paring knife, score the ends of each tomato with an "x" carefully, to avoid going too deep. Heat a pot of water to a boil and salt aggressively. Drop the tomatoes in the water and blanch for about 30 seconds, then strain tomatoes and drop directly into a bowl of ice water. When fully cooled, peel skins off tomatoes and cut into quarters, removing the center and the seeds. Dice tomatoes evenly and set aside. Heat a heavy-bottomed saucepot and add olive oil, which should become hot but not smoking. Add onions and garlic and cook evenly until translucent, with no color. Add the tomatoes and rest of ingredients and bring them to a boil, then reduce heat to low and cook about 30 minutes, until the liquid has evaporated and the jam has a glossy, thick consistency. Season to taste with salt and spread on a sheet tray to cool. When cool transfer to a Ball jar or other container with a lid and put in the fridge until ready to use.

To make the burrata: Cut the mozzarella curd in half, setting one half aside. Grate the other half with a cheese grater into a bowl and mix well with the cream until smooth and creamy and completely incorporated. Season to taste with salt and fresh cracked black pepper. When filling is done, put in fridge until ready to use and heat a pot of water to a boil. When water is boiling, turn heat off, and wait five minutes. When water is just cool enough to be able to touch with bare hands, drop the remaining half of mozzarella into the water. After about 5 minutes, remove with tongs and press flat against your hand with the other hand. Take the mozzarella in both hands and stretch across one hand until even, and using an ice cream scoop, scoop a heaping amount of the filling into the center of the cheese. Stretch the cheese around the filling, pulling it toward the center of the filling until completely stuffed. Once all four sides are stretched, the mozzarella will cool and seal itself. Flip the burrata over and place on a plate, which will further seal it.

To make the basil salt: Put all ingredients into a food processor and pulse until bright green and aromatic, about 20 seconds. Will keep for about 3 days in the fridge.

To serve: Spoon tomato jam over the top of the burrata, sprinkle with basil salt, and finish with a drizzle of olive oil. The leftover jam and salt can both be stored in Ball jars in the fridge for up to a week.

# Arancini Bros.

940 Flushing Avenue, Bushwick
(718) 418-6347
ARANCINIBROS.COM
Owner: Dave Campaniello

Insert your own ball jokes here.

There's nothing you can say about Arancini Bros. that owner Dave Campaniello hasn't already said himself. After all, the official slogan of his single-minded Bushwick business is "We've Got Balls." And Arancini Bros. really does have some mighty fine (ahem). It should, considering it's the first and only NYC eatery devoted entirely to the Sicilian street food—deep-fried "little oranges" made with Arborio rice and stuffed with a variety of fillings. "To be honest, the concept arose mainly from my own limitations—not being a trained chef," admits Campaniello, a former sound engineer. "I didn't feel qualified to open a full-blown restaurant. But being specialized in something enables me to concentrate on just one thing, and do it really well. You'd be amazed with how much versatility and creativity such a simple concept allows."

He's not kidding. In addition to the classic meat *ragù,* Campaniello rotates through over thirty types of arancini on any given day . . . think Philly cheesesteak, chicken marsala, roasted beets with goat cheese, white bean and escarole, and even an assortment of dessert options, like Nutella, strawberry mascarpone, and peanut butter mousse with chocolate.

In fact, Campaniello's balls have become so popular, he's contracted them out to both Yankee Stadium and Madison Square Garden. Both are places he never could have imagined being in just a few years ago . . . except maybe on the other side of a soundboard, that is. "Growing up, I always worked in restaurants, because it was something I knew. When my father moved to the United States from Italy in the 1970s, he spent years working in various restaurants in NYC," Campaniello began. "The ironic thing is, the food industry was always something I was trying to pull away from. I saw what the business was like and I didn't want to have any part of it!"

# ARANCINI AL RAGÙ

(MAKES ABOUT 15 ARANCINI)

*For the rice:*

6 cups beef stock
2 tablespoons unsalted butter
1 teaspoon sea salt
½ teaspoon saffron strands
2½ cups Arborio rice
½ cup grated Parmesan
½ cup grated pecorino

*For the ragù:*

1 pound ground beef
8 ounces ground pork
Sea salt and freshly ground pepper
4 ounces pancetta, finely chopped
1 teaspoon olive oil
1 small yellow onion, finely chopped
1 small carrot, finely chopped
1 celery stick, finely chopped
1 bay leaf
½ cup white wine
1 cup tomato puree
2 tablespoons tomato paste dissolved in
    1 cup warm water
¾ cup peas
1 tablespoon unsalted butter

*For the filling:*

8 ounces mozzarella, cut into ¼-inch cubes

*For the batter and breading:*

1½ cups flour
Salt
2 cups plain bread crumbs
Canola oil, for frying

In a medium saucepot over high heat, add the beef stock, butter, salt, and saffron. When the stock reaches a boil, add the rice and stir it a bit to prevent sticking. Let it come to a rolling boil and lower the heat a bit to medium. Stir the rice once in a while. You want the rice to absorb all of the liquid, which should take 15–20 minutes. Taste the rice; it should be slightly al dente but creamy. Remove the pot from the heat, add the cheeses, and stir well. Pour the rice onto a baking sheet and spread into a thin layer. Cover with plastic wrap and let cool, preferably overnight in the fridge.

Mix the ground beef and pork together with your hands and add salt and pepper generously. Set aside.

In a medium saucepot over medium-low heat, sauté the pancetta with the olive oil until the fat is melted. Add the onions and let cook until soft, about 5 minutes. Add the carrot and celery along with the bay leaf and cook until soft, 7–10 minutes.

Add the ground meat and turn the heat to high. Keep mixing with a wooden spoon until the meat is well done and browned. Add the white wine and stir until it is evaporated. Add the tomato puree and tomato paste in water. Bring to a boil, and then reduce the heat to low, stirring occasionally. There will be some fat that comes to the top. Skim it off with a ladle, but you want to leave some for the flavor. Let cook for about 1½ hours.

About 5 minutes before the ragù is done, sauté the peas in the butter with a pinch of salt and add to the ragù. Put the ragù in a bowl and set aside to cool. You can leave it overnight covered in the fridge.

Portion out cooled rice into identical portions. We weigh ours to 1.6 ounces. Take one portion and form it into a half sphere in the palm of your hand, making a cup-like shape to place the ragù and mozzarella into. Scoop a generous amount of ragù, about 2 teaspoons, into the half ball and then a few cubes of mozzarella. Take another portion of rice and flatten it into a disk shape. Place that disk over the half ball to enclose the ragù and cheese in the center. Have a bowl of warm water nearby to dip your hands into—it'll make the process easier and less sticky. Roll the ball around to enclose all ingredients in the center and shape into a perfectly round ball. Repeat with the remaining ingredients.

Place the flour and 1½ cups cold water into a bowl and add a pinch of salt. Mix with a whisk until smooth and about the consistency of eggnog. Add the bread crumbs to a large bowl or baking dish. Roll each rice ball in the batter and shake off excess batter. Then roll each ball in the bread crumbs. Repeat with all the balls.

Fill a heavy-duty pot with enough canola oil to submerge the balls in. Make sure the oil isn't near the top of the pot because it will overflow when you drop your balls in. Bring the oil to 350°F, using a high-temperature thermometer if you have one. If not, you can throw a small piece of white bread in to test; it should brown quickly and float when the oil is hot enough.

Use a slotted spoon or wire basket to lower your balls into the hot oil. Don't overcrowd the balls— maybe two or three at a time. Fry in batches until they are golden like arancini ("little oranges"), about 5 minutes. Remove and place on paper towels to drain. Eat hot.

# Arthur on Smith

276 Smith Street, Carroll Gardens
(718) 360-2340
ARTHURONSMITH.COM
Chef/Owner: Joe Isidori

Michelin-starred chef Joe Isidori never expected to find himself cooking his father's food. And yet, Arthur on Smith is a living ode to his late father, from the name (his dad's) to the home-style menu to the sepia-toned photos lining the walls. "Growing up, all I wanted to do was work for my father. At five years old, he had me cleaning squid and shrimp in his restaurants," Isidori laughs. "By the time I was twelve, I worked during the day as a prep cook and at night as a busboy. At seventeen I went into the kitchen full-time. And at nineteen I was accepted to the Culinary Institute of America, and decided I never wanted to cook Italian food again."

It wasn't until after his father's funeral, gathered at his restaurant eating Italian-American food, that Isidori had a true change of heart. "My business partners turned to me and said, 'Why the hell don't you cook this food? Don't you know how to do this?'" Isidori remembers. "And I said, 'Of course I do, but I don't want to. This is my dad's food.' And they're like, 'You're stupid, you're crazy.' They were right. So I came up with this idea."

At Arthur on Smith, Isidori applies his own modern, fine-dining aesthetic to his father's old-school recipes. Take the handmade pappardelle, topped with a refined Bolognese of fresh lamb sausage that's been spiced with *urfa biber,* a dried, Turkish pepper. "I add small, innovative touches, little right-hand turns that make the dishes sing a little bit," says Isidori. "I've actually coined a term for what we're doing . . . New American Italian. Kind of like Patsy's meets The French Laundry."

# LAMB SAUSAGE WITH PAPPARDELLE

### (SERVES 4)

Chef's Note: Urfa biber can be found online or at well-stocked middle eastern markets, like Sahadi's.

1½ teaspoons cumin seed

1 teaspoon fennel seed

2 tablespoons urfa biber

1 pound ground lamb

1 teaspoon black pepper (approximately 10–12 twists of a pepper mill)

6 teaspoons plus 2 teaspoons kosher salt

4 fresh sage leaves

1 pound fresh pappardelle pasta

⅓ cup grated pecorino cheese

Toast cumin and fennel seed together in a skillet until aromatic. Grind in a spice grinder until coarse. Add mixture to urfa biber.

Combine seasoning mixture to ground lamb in large mixing bowl. Divide equally into four patties.

Bring 6-quart pot of water to a boil. Add 6 teaspoons kosher salt to water. (General rule of thumb is 1 teaspoon per quart of water—it should taste like ocean water.)

Season patties with remaining salt and black pepper. Sear patties in sauté pan until dark golden color is achieved. Add sage leaves and cook on both sides till crisp. Remove and reserve. Flip over sausage and cook until same golden color is achieved. Break sausage with a wooden spatula into small meatball-like pieces. Add 2-ounce ladle of pasta water to deglaze pan. This saves the meat flavor that developed from searing. Remove from heat.

Place fresh pappardelle in a pasta basket and cook in the seasoned boiling water. Cook for approximately 2–3 minutes. You want it cooked with a little bit of tooth (or resistance) remaining as it will be finished in the sauté pan with the sausage. Be sure to give the pasta a gentle stir at 1 minute to prevent sticking in the water.

Place the sausage back on heat. Lift the pasta basket to drain pasta and add it to the heated sausage. Add the grated pecorino and gently toss the pasta and sausage. You are looking to emulsify to the pecorino with the cooking liquid to achieve a nice thickly coated pasta.

Serve pasta in four bowls or one bowl for family style. Garnish each serving with crisp sage leaves.

# THE ORIGINAL NATHAN'S FAMOUS

Most people's experience with Nathan's is limited to a withered hot dog from a strip-mall food court, or a box of flaccid french fries at some rest stop off of the interstate. And that's a shame. Because those subpar franchises have very little to do with the real Nathan's Famous, which has stood at the corner of Surf Avenue and Stillwell on Coney Island since 1916. Nathan Handwerker, a young Polish immigrant, used his $300 life savings to open the nickel hot dog stand, to the encouragement of his singing waiter friends Eddie Cantor and Jimmy Durante. And the original recipe for those franks, provided by his fiancée, Ida, remains largely the same today (unfortunately, we can't say the same for the price.) The natural-casing, all-beef hot dogs are prepared on a griddle, expertly seasoned by years of use, as opposed to the hit-or-miss franchises, which often throw their skinless franks on a roller grill. The flagship restaurant also plays host to one of Brooklyn's most enduring traditions, the Fourth of July Hot Dog Eating Contest, where reigning champ Joey Chestnut famously set a record for sixty-eight HD&B (sixty-eight hot dogs and buns eaten in 10 minutes.) While that's not a feat we're interested in challenging anytime soon (two dogs with mustard and kraut, medium fries, and a large lemonade is good enough for us), there's no denying—a summer in Brooklyn just wouldn't be the same without Nathan's Famous, a true Coney Island original.

# BARK HOT DOGS

474 BERGEN STREET, PARK SLOPE
(718) 789-1939
BARKHOTDOGS.COM
OWNER: JOSHUA SHARKEY

It may seem like sacrilege to attempt to "gourmetize" hot dogs, one of Brooklyn's most iconic foods. And certainly, Bark makes no bones about listing all of their virtuous purveyors, from Hartmann's Old World Sausage, who makes their private-label dogs, to Deep Root Cooperative, which supplies the cabbage and carrots for coleslaw, and Hawthorne Valley Farm, which keeps the eatery in lacto-fermented sauerkraut.

But at its core, Bark Hot Dogs remains resolutely straightforward and traditional—pork-and-beef franks, mustard, ketchup, onions, kraut, pickles, chili, relish—albeit mostly made in-house, and with ingredients that are a cut above. "We're not being gimmicky about it. We don't have off-the-wall, frou-frou toppings," promises owner Joshua Sharkey. "But instead of using cheap canned beans for our baked beans, we use really great heirlooms and quality smoked pork. It's about taking time-honored items and adding terrific ingredients and skillful technique."

More than anything, Bark has attempted to use cleaned-up, fast-casual cuisine to promote the notion of healthy living, demonstrating that food doesn't have to be mass-produced and processed in order to be tasty, simple, and affordable. "No, you don't get a two-dollar hot dog here, but you're also not spending eighteen dollars for a sausage. We're sort of the in-between, trying to get everyone to understand the importance of eating well on every level."

Helming a popular hot-dog stand has certainly been an eye-opening experience for Sharkey, a classically trained chef who came up in high-end restaurants like Cafe Gray. "When we first opened, we had an item called the NYC Dog, and customers were really passionate about the fact that it wasn't really a NYC dog, because it had to have this or that," Sharkey remembers, laughing (incidentally, the frank currently boasts homemade sweet and sour onions and yellow mustard). "In the fine-dining world, you control the experience, you tell everyone what to eat. But here, at Bark, the customers are the experts. It's definitely been a huge change from what I'm used to!"

# Beef Chili

(SERVES 6)

¾ pound brisket, ground

¾ pound beef short rib, ground

2 tablespoons ancho chile powder

2 tablespoons grape-seed or canola oil

1½ tablespoons sea salt to taste

10 cloves garlic, finely chopped

1 large onion, finely chopped

¼ cup cider vinegar

2 tablespoons dark brown sugar

1 tablespoon paprika

Pinch cayenne pepper to taste

1 cup canned crushed San Marzano tomatoes

¼ cup water

Season the ground meat with the chile powder. Heat a large pan on high heat, then add the oil. When the oil is hot, add the meat to the pan and sear it until it is deep golden brown. Remove meat from the pan and reserve, leaving a little of the fat in the pan. Season the meat with ½ tablespoon of the salt. Turn the heat down on the pan, and add the garlic. Cook the garlic in the leftover beef fat, making sure not to brown it, about 1 minute. Add the onion and ½ tablespoon of the salt and sauté, making sure not to brown it. Once the onion is completely soft, add all of the remaining ingredients. Add the meat back to the pan. Bring everything to a simmer, simmering slowly for about 1–1½ hours, until the meat is completely tender. Serve warm.

# Sweet Pickle Slaw

(MAKES ABOUT 4 CUPS)

*For the dressing:*

2½ cups mayonnaise

2 tablespoons cider vinegar

¾ cup pickle juice

1 teaspoon sugar

1 teaspoon salt

½ teaspoon celery seed

*For the slaw:*

½ cup shredded carrot

3 cups cabbage, sliced thin

1 teaspoon salt

¼ teaspoon sugar

½ cup cole slaw dressing

Mix all of the ingredients for the dressing together in a bowl and reserve.

Mix the carrot and cabbage together and toss with salt and sugar. Let sit for at least 4 hours, then drain and squeeze out all of the liquid. Mix dressing and the drained vegetables together and serve.

# BELLI OSTERIA

860 FULTON STREET, CLINTON HILL
(347) 799-1230
BELLIBROOKLYN-HUB.COM
CHEF/OWNER: ANDRES RODAS
OWNER: ANDRES WHANG

Who would have guessed that an Argentina-born Queens resident would become such a proponent of Italian food in Brooklyn?

"Many people don't know this, but the majority of the Argentinean population actually comes from Italy," says Andres Rodas, owner of Fragole in Carroll Gardens, Piccoli in Windsor Terrace, Piccoli Trattoria in Park Slope, and the new Belli Osteria, part of a growing foodie renaissance in Clinton Hill. "If you go to any restaurant, pasta is half the menu. And every neighborhood has two or three stores that sell fresh pasta, with lines out the door every Sunday."

That makes it a safe bet to go for the noodles at Belli, like pappardelle, fettuccine, and fat little gnudi, which are made in-house each day. But even though the food is more recognizably Mediterranean in influence, Rodas hopes to best distinguish his restaurant with a liberal dose of South American hospitality.

"One of the things that shocked me when I first moved from Argentina and began working at high-end restaurants in the city is that they try to pull you in and then push

you out the door," Rodas says. "That's why I eventually opened a restaurant in Brooklyn, which is very similar to the neighborhood in Argentina where I grew up. You walk down the street and you feel like a rock star because everybody knows you."

"We want this to be a community—a place where people come, chat with the neighbors at the table next to them, and share their wine," he continues. "We welcome you here. Our customers are like friends."

## GNUDI WITH ZUCCHINI, BUTTER & ROSEMARY

### (SERVES 6–8)

Chef's Note: Gnudi means "nude "in Italian. They are filling without feeling heavy. They are called "nude" because they are like ravioli without the dough.

*For the gnudi:*

1 pound fresh ricotta cheese

⅓ cup freshly grated Parmigiano Reggiano, plus extra for garnish

1 tablespoon unsalted butter, melted

1 large egg, lightly beaten

½ teaspoon ground nutmeg

1 teaspoon minced fresh sage (optional)

1 cup all-purpose flour

4 cups semolina

5 tablespoons salt

*For the sauce:*

2 tablespoons olive oil

2 garlic cloves (whole)

2 zucchinis, diced

6 tablespoons unsalted butter at room temperature

1 teaspoon rosemary leaves

To make the gnudi: Combine the first 6 ingredients in a large mixing bowl with a rubber spatula. Fold gently until all the ingredients come together. Next, fold in the cup of flour until it is combined with the ricotta mixture, adding more flour by the tablespoon if needed so that the mixture isn't too sticky and all the flour has been absorbed. Dust a baking sheet with semolina. Gently tear pieces of dough and roll them between your hands to make 1-inch balls and put them on tray dusted with semolina. Cover and refrigerate for up to 10 hours, or freeze for up to 3 weeks.

Fill a large stockpot with 6 quarts of water and add 5 tablespoons of salt. Bring the water to boil over high heat. In a skillet, heat the olive oil until smoking, add the garlic cloves and shake the skillet for about 30 seconds, then add the zucchini and let it brown for about 3 minutes, shaking the pan at 1-minute intervals. Add the butter and rosemary and let the butter foam for a few moments. Don't overcook, to avoid introducing any bitter flavor.

Add the gnudi to the boiling water. When they just float to the surface (in about 3–4 minutes), remove with a slotted spoon to drain and add to the sauce. Cook the pasta with the sauce for about 2 minutes, stirring with a rubber spatula avoiding smashing the gnudi. (Add some fresh water if necessary to keep the sauce from drying out). Divide the gnudi among the plates and sprinkle with a good amount of Parmigiano Reggiano.

# Risotto with Braised Red Onions, Moscato & Gorgonzola Dolce

### (SERVES 4–5)

Chef's Note: The secret to the best risotto is first toasting the rice until it starts to crackle slightly, and giving an energetic stirring at the end of the cooking process to release the starches in the rice.

*For the braised onions:*

3 medium red onions, trimmed, halved vertically,
    and cut into ⅔-inch wedges
3 dried bay leaves, each torn into 3 pieces
3 tablespoons extra-virgin olive oil
1½ tablespoons apple cider vinegar
1 tablespoon dry white wine (like Pinot Grigio
    or Sauvignon Blanc)
1 teaspoon Kosher salt

*For the risotto:*

6–7 cups vegetable broth or light chicken broth
1 stick unsalted butter
2 shallots, peeled and finely chopped
2 cups Arborio or Carnaroli rice
⅓ cup dry white wine
⅓ cup dry Moscato wine
½ cup freshly grated Parmesan cheese
Sea salt and freshly ground black pepper
4 thin slices hard Gorgonzola cheese
    (almost crumbled slices)

Position a rack in the center of the oven and heat the oven to 375°F. Arrange the onion wedges in an overlapping single layer in a shallow 10 x 15-inch baking dish. Top with bay leaves. In a small bowl, mix the olive oil, vinegar, white wine, and 1½ tablespoons water, and drizzle over the onions. Sprinkle evenly with salt. Cover the

baking dish tightly with aluminum foil. Braise the onions in the oven until completely tender when pierced close to the root ends with a fork, about 45 minutes. Uncover the dish and continue to braise until all of the liquid has evaporated and the onions are darkly roasted and glossy, about 20 minutes.

Put the broth in a saucepan set over medium heat and keep at a gentle simmer. Melt half the butter in a large, heavy saucepan and add the shallots. Cook gently for about 4 minutes until soft but not browned. Add the rice and stir until well coated with butter and the rice starts to crackle slightly. Pour in the wines and boil hard until it has reduced and the alcohol has evaporated. Add 1 ladle of hot broth and simmer, stirring until it has been absorbed. Repeat. After 10 minutes add the braised onions and mix well. Continue to add the broth at intervals for about 8 more minutes, until the broth has been absorbed and the rice is tender but firm. Turn off the heat and add the other half of the butter, Parmesan cheese, and salt and pepper to taste. Stir well to release the starch in the grains of rice (this is called *mantecare*) until the risotto starts becoming creamy (about 1 minute).

Spoon into warmed bowls and top each plate with 1 slice of Gorgonzola cheese and drizzle with best extra-virgin olive oil you can get. Serve immediately.

# 6-HOUR STOUT-BRAISED PORK SHANK
## WITH CREAMY POLENTA

(SERVES 4)

Chef's Note: A simple braise inspired by a great Brooklyn Black Chocolate Stout. Pork shanks are a delicious and inexpensive cut that can yield a memorable meal with little effort after a nice long time in a low oven.

*For the braised pork:*

1 tablespoon vegetable oil
4 pork shanks
Kosher salt and cracked black pepper
1 onion, finely chopped
2 ribs celery, finely chopped
2 bay leaves
2 sprigs thyme
1 sprig rosemary
¼ cup dried wild mushrooms, rinsed in
   warm water
1 cup stout beer or similar style
3 cups chicken stock or beef stock
1 tablespoon butter

*For the polenta:*

1½ cups whole milk
3 cups cold water
Pinch of sea salt
1 cup fine ground polenta
¼ teaspoon white pepper
½ cup shredded fontina cheese
⅓ cup grated Parmesan cheese

To make the pork: Preheat the oven to 220°F. Heat the oil in large heavy pan over medium heat. Wipe the pieces of meat dry. Season pork shank with salt and pepper. Brown the pork shanks evenly and gently on all sides, about 3 minutes per side. Pour off excess fat. Rearrange the meat in the pan. Add the onions, celery, bay leaves, thyme, rosemary, mushrooms, the beer and the stock. Bring to a simmer, cover with aluminum foil, and place in the oven for about 5–6 hours, until fork tender. With a slotted spoon, remove the shanks. Handle them carefully at this point, as they will tend to fall apart. Cover loosely with foil to keep warm. Strain the braising liquid into a saucepan, pushing down the vegetables and herbs to extract all the juices. Skim the surface fat from the strained liquid and bring to a simmer over medium-high heat, and keep skimming a few more times, until it is reduced by a third (about 15 minutes). Add butter to the simmering sauce and stir for 1 minute.

To make the polenta: In a large, heavy pan combine the first 3 ingredients. Bring to a boil and reduce the heat to low. Gradually whisk in the polenta, and keep whisking so the polenta doesn't scorch. After a few minutes switch to a wooden spoon and stir every few minutes until the polenta is creamy (about 15 minutes). Remove from the heat and stir in the white pepper, fontina, and Parmesan cheese.

To serve: Put about 1½ cups of fresh polenta on each plate, top with 1 shank per plate, and spoon some sauce over the meat.

# BEP

346 BEDFORD AVENUE, WILLIAMSBURG
(718) 218-7067
BEPRESTAURANT.BLOGSPOT.COM
OWNER: AN NGUYEN XUAN

If Smorgasburg stands and food trucks have become rites of passage for fledgling foodie businesses in Brooklyn, Bep's An Nguyen Xuan is paving the way for the pop-up.

"The economy crashed just when I was looking to open up a restaurant," says the young Vietnamese chef, who was born and raised in Paris, France. "I was walking by Simple Cafe in Williamsburg one Monday, and noticed it was closed. I asked the owners if I could use their restaurant for that one day, and they liked the idea. And so have the customers. People get very excited about new things."

They've been so eager, in fact, that Bep now serves dinner five days a week—chopsticks and bottles of hot sauce lining the tables from 5 p.m. on, and Simple Cafe staples like quinoa salad and *croque monsieur* giving way to *bánh mì, cha giò,* and beef *pho.*

"The other great thing about this is that you get to constantly reinvent yourself," says Xuan. "I can do Thai dishes one day, Vietnamese the next, and French the next. It gives you a lot of flexibility, both in scheduling and what you can do."

That includes adding sophisticated flourishes to classic country staples like *bun cha ca,* the famous dish from Hanoi. "In Vietnam, every restaurant serves one single dish. So if you want turmeric catfish with dill, you go to Cha Ca La Vong," he explains. "All of the ingredients are served separately there . . . fish, noodles, herbs, fish sauce, shrimp paste. But my twist is to put them all together with a fish dipping sauce, topped with a crispy black sesame cracker."

# Bun Chá Cá

(SERVES 4–6)

4–5 fillets of catfish or basa cut into 2-inch pieces

1 package of dry rice vermicelli noodles

2 teaspoons vegetable or canola oil

1 bunch fresh dill, coarsely chopped, thick stems removed (set some aside for garnish)

3 scallions, coarsely chopped

½ cup coarsely crushed unsalted dry-roasted peanuts

½ English cucumber, thinly sliced

1 black sesame rice cracker

*For the Vietnamese fish sauce dressing:*

½ cup water

2 tablespoons sugar

Juice of 2 limes

3 cloves minced garlic (use more or less according to taste)

⅛ cup fish sauce, adjust to taste

1 tablespoon rice or plain vinegar (optional)

1 Thai chile, finely chopped (optional)

*For the fish marinade:*

1 tablespoon shrimp paste

2 tablespoons turmeric powder

2 tablespoons vegetable or canola oil

*For the pickled onions:*

1 teaspoon sugar

2 teaspoons vinegar

1 medium red onion, thinly sliced

In a large bowl or container, mix all ingredients for the Vietnamese fish sauce dressing, and set aside.

Combine the shrimp paste, turmeric, and oil in a large bowl and mix well. Add catfish/basa pieces and mix gently but thoroughly. Allow the fish to marinate in the fridge for 1 hour.

In the meantime, cook the vermicelli noodles according to the directions on the package. Be sure to rinse noodles in cold water to stop the cooking process and drain thoroughly. Set aside to cool.

Pickle the red onions. In a small bowl, mix sugar and vinegar. Add the thinly sliced onions and let them sit for at least 10 minutes.

Cook sesame cracker in microwave for 1–2 minutes, or until fully expanded and crispy. Precooked crackers may also be found in some Asian markets.

Cook the fish in 3–4 batches. Pour oil into a heated wok. Once the oil is hot, add a quarter of the fish. After 30 seconds, reduce the heat to medium and let the fish cook for 2–3 minutes on each side or until golden. Remove wok from heat and add a handful of dill and chopped scallions. Mix gently in the wok then set aside on a plate. Continue the same process with the rest of the fish.

To present the dish, put desired amount of vermicelli into a bowl and create a small dip in the center using your fingers. Into the dip, add mixture of fish, dill, and scallions. Top with pickled onions, crushed peanuts, sliced cucumbers, and black sesame cracker. Garnish with lots of fresh dill.

Dress with Vietnamese fish sauce dressing according to your liking.

# BEVACCO

60 HENRY STREET, BROOKLYN HEIGHTS
(718) 624-1444
BEVACCO.COM
CHEF: CHIARA ZAGO

It's an odd thing about Brooklyn Heights. Although it's long been one of the most lusted-after neighborhoods in Brooklyn, with its multimillion dollar brownstones, leafy streets, and proximity to the promenade, it's also equally distinguished by its surprising dearth of restaurants. That's what's made the two-year-old Bevacco such a welcome addition to the area; a classy alternative to the franchises and chains ringing the courthouse and often uninspiring eateries lining Montague Street.

"It's true that the cultural dynamic in Brooklyn Heights is not as varied in ethnicity as in other parts of the city. And I think that this has slowed down the diversity of food here, which has translated to fewer choices regarding restaurants," theorizes chef Chiara Zago. "I think it's also made many people in this neighborhood less adventurous foodwise, but that's changing. There is an emerging food scene here unlike in Williamsburg, where I live, which is oversaturated with restaurants!"

Not content to be just another boring neighborhood red-sauce joint, Zago adds a New American spin to classic Mediterranean dishes at Bevacco, sourcing ingredients like burrata from Wisconsin, and heirloom tomatoes, breakfast radishes, kale, peas, beets, and tatsoi greens from nearby farms. "I've been able to incorporate these wonderful local products into a modern view of Italian cuisine," Zago says. "I also want to introduce Venetian-style food to the bar menu, which we call Cicchetti . . . small portions that are enjoyed with wine. It's a tradition that goes back to the 1400s."

# SPIEDINI DI BRANZINO WITH SPINACH, BEET MASHED POTATOES & GREEN PEA SAUCE

(SERVES 4)

*For fish skewers:*

Branzino or striped bass, one 10-ounce fillet
   portion per serving
2 red peppers, cored and cut into wide strips
1 red onion, halved and cut into strips
8 spears medium asparagus
8 fresh bay leaves
Extra-virgin olive oil
Flour for light dusting

*For sautéed spinach:*

6 tablespoons extra virgin olive oil
4 cloves garlic, smashed
1 pound washed baby spinach

*For beet mashed potatoes:*

1 pound Idaho potatoes, peeled and quartered
1 small boiled or roasted red beet, peeled
6 ounces milk
2 ounces (4 tablespoons) butter
2 ounces grated Parmesan cheese

*For green pea sauce:*

2 shallots, chopped into fine dice
4 tablespoons extra-virgin olive oil
1 pound fresh or frozen green peas
2 cups vegetable stock
1 sprig mint leaves
Salt and pepper

For the fish skewers: Preheat oven to 360°F. Discard the skin from the fish fillets. With a small, sharp knife, make a small hole in each fish fillet, red pepper strip, onion strip, and bay leaf. Using the asparagus as a skewer, alternate fish, red pepper, onion, and bay leaves (factor two skewers per person). In an ovenproof pan, heat oil until just hot. Lightly dredge skewers in flour, gently shaking off any excess (this prevents the skewers from sticking to the pan). Lightly cook one side on top of stove, and finish in oven for 6 or 7 minutes, depending on thickness of fish.

For the spinach: Heat oil in sauté pan with smashed cloves of garlic. When the garlic turns golden, remove and set aside. Add the spinach to the flavored oil and sauté until wilted.

For the potatoes: Boil potatoes until tender. Combine milk and butter and heat until warm (do not boil).

Place potatoes, beet, milk, butter, and cheese in food processor. Pulse just until smooth, being careful not to overprocess, as potatoes will turn gluey.

For the pea sauce: In a deep sauté pan, sauté shallot in the olive oil over low heat until translucent. Add peas, vegetable stock to cover, mint, and salt and pepper to taste. When the peas are soft, blend all and strain. This will be a concentrated sauce.

Plate fish skewers with a serving of spinach and potatoes, and drizzle with pea sauce.

# BiteMe Cheesecakes

27 North 6th Street, Williamsburg (Smorgasburg)
(551) 574-0840
BITEMECHEESECAKES.COM
Chef/Owner: Tyreece Johnson
Owner: Justice Hall

Brooklyn's favorite dessert has been downsized.

"You know how you buy one of those big globs of cheesecake and then you can only have so much of it?" questions Tyreece Johnson, chef and co-owner of the diminutive dessert company BiteMe Cheesecakes. "You don't get bored with these. Two bites of cake and you're ready to try something else."

Not that we haven't happily eaten our way through oversized slabs of Junior's iconic cherry cheesecake before (and gone back for seconds). But Johnson is definitely onto

something. Instead of overtaxing one's taste buds with a single, tooth-numbingly sweet flavor, it's a pleasure to graze through a number of unique options, like peanut butter and jelly, sweet potato rum crunch, apple bacon, and limoncello meringue. And locals agree—in addition to doing a steady business online, BiteMe Cheesecakes has become a popular dessert stop at Smorgasburg. "You're able to express who are you as a chef or restaurateur without making a huge investment," Johnson says of the benefits of the weekend food festival. "You can find out if your business plan works or not, and build a fan base. I mean, look at People's Pops and Mighty Quinn Barbecue, which have blown up because of Smorgasburg."

Since Johnson is working on steadily growing his brand, the recipe for those tasty, palm-size cakes remains a secret. But he promises that his two most ordered toppings—strawberry balsamic reduction and Merlot compote—will become go-to items in your home kitchen, whether poured on pancakes and waffles or dolloped on ice cream and peanut butter sandwiches. "I've actually made spiked lemonade with them too. Add two tablespoons to lemonade, along with a little vodka. It's really refreshing," insists Johnson. "They're so versatile, it's a shame to just save them for cheesecake!"

# STRAWBERRY REDUCTION

(MAKES 14–15 OUNCES OF SAUCE)

1 pound strawberries
4 tablespoons sugar
2 tablespoons balsamic vinegar
2 tablespoons Sauvignon Blanc
1 tablespoon fresh lemon juice (optional)

Cut strawberries into half-inch slices. Mix in the remaining ingredients and let stand for 30 minutes. Pour the strawberries in a saucepan and bring to a boil. Once the strawberries start to boil, reduce to a simmer. When the strawberries have cooked down by a quarter to a half (this depends how thick you prefer it), remove from heat and allow it to cool.

# MERLOT COMPOTE

(MAKES 14 OUNCES OF COMPOTE)

8 ounces blueberries
8 ounces blackberries
4 tablespoons sugar
½ teaspoon cinnamon
¼ teaspoon nutmeg
2 tablespoons Merlot

Mix all ingredients and let stand for 30 minutes. Pour the berries into a sauce pan and bring to a boil. Once the berries start to boil, reduce to a simmer. Cook sauce down until slightly thick. Allow time to cool. Now serve over ice cream, pancakes, and of course cheesecakes.

# BROOKLYN BRINE

574A PRESIDENT STREET, GOWANUS
(347) 223-4345
BROOKLYNBRINECO.COM
OWNER: SHAMUS JONES

There are plenty of restaurant trends with an understandably high hip factor. Spicy sriracha? Definitely cool. Creative cupcakes? Cute, but cool. Anything cocktail-related? Invariably in vogue. But pickles? How did a foodstuff associated with Jewish delis and tiny ethnic markets become all the rage with Brooklyn's artisanal elite? "The cross-cultural population in Brooklyn has led to an innate familiarity with pickling. Somebody's Bubby taught them how to do it, or they have memories of going to Essex Street and getting a Guss' pickle," theorizes Shamus Jones, a Midwood native and the owner of Brooklyn Brine. "And since it's a very easy thing to make yourself, the barrier entry to starting a pickle company is very low."

Not that Jones, a classically trained chef, is in the habit of simply sticking bushels of kirbys into vats of vinegar and calling it a day (or a business). In addition to classic cucumber variations like NYC Deli, maple bread and butter, and Damn Spicy (liberally

studded with whole, organic chiles), Brooklyn Brine specializes in inventive fermented veggies, like chipotle carrots, Moroccan beans, whiskey-barrel sauerkraut and lavender asparagus. "I was able to carve out a pretty unique place. We're also the first to have a line of spirit-infused pickles, using Dogfish Head Ale, and gin from Finger Lakes Distilling," Jones says.

Perhaps the thing that Jones has preserved most effectively at Brooklyn Brine, however, is the ancient art of pickling itself. "Somewhere along the line, pickles became commoditized, mass-produced items, made with unnatural preservatives, crisping agents, corn syrup, and food coloring," Jones says. "I think that it was a long time coming, people wanting a better-made pickle. And they've also realized that this staple pantry item can really be taken to the next level." He smiles. "So maybe that explains what's so hip about pickling."

# ROSEMARY LEMON BEETS WITH GIN

### (MAKES 5 16-OUNCE JARS WITH LIDS)

*For the rosemary-preserved lemons:*

3 lemons, halved

2 sprigs rosemary

2 tablespoons sea salt

Cheesecloth

*For the beets:*

3 golden beets, medium to small

1 tablespoon plus ¼ cup sea salt

1 quart apple cider vinegar

⅛ cup cane sugar

¼ cup gin (Brooklyn Brine uses Seneca Drums Gin from Finger Lakes Distilling, fingerlakesdistilling.com)

2 tablespoons dried lavender

4 teaspoons black peppercorns

2 tablespoons coriander seeds

2 tablespoons yellow mustard seeds

4 sprigs tarragon

2 sprigs rosemary, cut in half

2 medium shallots, thinly sliced

1 rosemary-preserved lemon, quartered, pith and pulp removed

To prep the jars: Wash in hot, soapy water (don't forget the lids) and drain. Place clean jars in a pot and add water to cover. Heat water to 180°F; keep jars hot until ready to fill.

To make the rosemary-preserved lemons: Squeeze juice from the lemons into the jar. Place rosemary sprigs in the jar and rest lemon halves on top. Cover top layer of lemons with salt and then press on the lemon peels, packing them tight and submerging them in the juice. Cover with cheesecloth and store in a cool, dark place

(but not the refrigerator). Check lemons in one week; they should smell sweet and lemony without sour notes.

To make the beets: Cook beets in large pot of boiling salted water until tender, about 10 minutes. Using slotted spoon, transfer beets to a colander and rinse with cold water. To peel, just ease the skin off with your fingers—no knife required. Set aside.

In a second pot (make sure it's nonreactive stainless steel), combine ¼ cup sea salt, vinegar, sugar, gin, lavender, and 1 quart water. Over high heat, bring liquid to 212°F and stir to dissolve the salt and sugar. Lower the heat to medium-low. Once the lavender is aromatic, about 5 minutes, strain the liquid, discarding the lavender.

Combine the dried spices in a bowl.

Using a jar lifter or long tongs, remove jars from hot water and drain. Add 1 tablespoon spice mixture, 1 sprig tarragon, ½ sprig rosemary, ½ shallot and ¼ rosemary-preserved lemon to each jar.

Halve beets, then slice ¼-inch thin across. Fill each jar 1 inch from the top.

Ladle brine into each jar, leaving ½-inch headspace. Wipe any spillover with a clean towel. Twist the lid snug.

In a large pot, bring water to a boil. Gently lower jars into water. Cover pot. Wait until the water returns to a rolling boil and then "cook" for 10 minutes. Uncover the pot and let the jars sit for a few minutes to allow the liquid inside to stabilize.

Place the jars on a cutting board or on a counter lined with a kitchen towel. Let sit 12–24 hours until the seal sets.

Press down on the lid: if the jar is properly sealed, the button top will be concave and the lid will not move. Keep unopened jars in a cool, dark place for up to 1 year.

# PICKLING IN BROOKLYN

Pickles have long been a staple of Brooklyn food culture, from kosher dills fished out of wooden barrels, deposited in a swatch of brown paper, and sold for a nickel, to half-sour spears accompanying corned beef sandwiches at Jewish delis, to sausage-stuffed cherry peppers peddled at Italian *salumerias*, and vats of vinegared beets, tomatoes, and mushrooms central to most Russian and Polish markets. So who would have ever predicted they'd become so trendy and cool? Easy and economical, pickling has been at the forefront of Brooklyn's DIY craze. Young food artisans are currently taking the time-honored art of fermentation into the twentieth century, infusing their pickles with contemporary flavor and flair. Check out the Smokra (smoked, pickled okra) at Rick's Picks (rickspicks.com), the flowering dill pickles at McClure's (mcclurespickles.com), and the curried squash or whiskey-barrel sauerkraut at Brooklyn Brine (see above). And homemade pickles are the pride of the house at restaurants like Mile End Deli in Boerum Hill (97A Hoyt Street; 718-852-7510; mileenddeli.com) where brightly colored jars of carrots, cauliflower, and beets line the shelves like edible pop art. Not that you can't still find seriously old-school cukes (giant vats and all) at places like Ess-a-Pickle in Borough Park (1470 39th Street; 917-701-4000) . . . a reincarnation of the hundred-year-old Guss' Pickles on the Lower East Side!

# BROOKLYN CURED

BROOKLYNCURED.COM
OWNER: SCOTT BRIDI

As a boy growing up in a food-obsessed family in Bensonhurst, Scott Bridi distinctly remembers tagging along on weekly runs to D. Coluccio and Sons to pick up fresh cheese, olives, and flour to make pasta. Which is why he never could have imagined that, years later, he would be supplying his own handmade charcuterie to A.L.C Italian Grocery in Bay Ridge. "It's incredibly meaningful to be selling sausages to Louis Coluccio," Bridi enthuses. "His family has this amazing shop that was so significant to my own family, and that connectivity is pretty much everything."

In fact, Brooklyn Cured's client list reads like a Who's Who of local retailers (Sahadi's, Eastern District, Stinky Bklyn, the Greene Grape), and restaurants (Bark Hot Dogs, Brooklyn Farmacy, Bonnie's Grill, 606 R&D), who've embraced Bridi's unimpeachable technique and Brooklyn-centric ethos. Take the hot Italian sausage, which Bridi describes as "a throwback to the old neighborhood"; the coriander-crusted pastrami, "this is how we do it in Brooklyn"; the spicy andouille, "the Holy Trinity meets the holiest borough"; and the country pâté, "from the rolling hills of Sunset Park." That would be in Industry City, the site of Brooklyn Cured's production facility. It's another thing Bridi never could have imagined while growing up . . . that a row of abandoned warehouses at the edge of a rough-around-the-edges neighborhood (known mostly for its prevalence of tiny taquerias and proximity to the Greenwood Cemetery) would become home base for many of the borough's top food artisans.

"Blue Marble, Liddabit Sweets, Robicelli's, The Good Batch—it's become such a hub for small businesses without too many resources," Bridi says. "We all share wholesale accounts and sourcing contacts. It's awesome to be involved in a community of people that have similar values and all make amazing food. They've definitely become some of our closest supporters and best friends."

# Country Pâté

### (MAKES 14 4-OUNCE PORTIONS)

3⅓ pounds ground pork butt (70% lean/30% fat)

1 pound ground pork liver (If you don't have access to a meat grinder, it's best to have your local butcher grind the pork butt and pork liver for you.)

5 tablespoons Diamond Crystal brand kosher salt (or 38 grams of any other salt)*

½ teaspoon pink salt (Optional—it's for appearance only. You can find it online at Butcher & Packer, butcher-packer.com.)

1 tablespoon black peppercorns, finely ground

1½ teaspoon granulated sugar

½ teaspoon ground allspice

¼ teaspoon cinnamon

Zest of ½ an orange

Zest of ½ a lemon

½ teaspoon thyme

1 teaspoon chopped rosemary

2 cloves garlic, minced

½ cup port wine

*The weight per volume of different brands of kosher salt varies wildly, so if you don't use Diamond, it's best to weigh the salt in grams rather than measure it with spoons. If you use the same number of tablespoons of another kosher salt or table salt, the pâté will be too salty.*

Preheat oven to 300°F. Combine all ingredients in a large bowl and mix by hand for about 5–6 minutes, until all ingredients are incorporated. Wear plastic gloves when you mix, otherwise it can get pretty messy. When you mix, be sure to fold the bottom of the mixture onto the top of it and repeat. Work it like pasta dough or bread dough for a bit. The pâté mixture will feel firmer the longer you mix it. This will create the structure that holds the pâté together.

Spray a 16 x 4-inch loaf pan generously with nonstick cooking spray. Press the pâté mixture tightly into the pan, about an inch at a time. Make sure there are no gaps within the mixture. If the pâté isn't pressed tightly, there will be cracks in the finished loaf.

Place the loaf pan in a baking pan with warm water coming halfway up the sides.

Cover pâté with aluminum foil after it starts to get golden brown on top (about 45 minutes into cooking time). Cook pâté to an internal temperature of 150°F. Use a meat thermometer to probe the center of the pâté to get its internal temperature. The total cooking time will be approximately 1½–2 hours.

Cool the pâté at room temperature before refrigerating. Refrigerate overnight. To remove from the loaf pan, gently trace a butter knife along the edges of the pâté. Turn the loaf pan upside down and tap the sides onto the counter or cutting board to remove the pâté.

Slice and eat with warm toasted bread or crackers and some mustard and pickles. The pâté holds in the refrigerator tightly wrapped in plastic for up to 1 week.

# Brooklyn Farmacy & Soda Fountain

513 Henry Street, Carroll Gardens
(718) 522-6260
brooklynfarmacy.blogspot.com
Owners: Peter Freeman and Gia Giasullo

Peter Freeman and Gia Giasullo are real jerks.

No, really, it says so right on their shirts. That's because the brother-sister team has revitalized one of Brooklyn's most beloved institutions, the classic ice cream parlor and soda fountain. "My mom always said I should open a diner or be a sixth-grade social studies teacher. And this is like a diner for sixth-graders," jokes Freeman.

"The Farm," as locals affectionately call it, faithfully re-creates each nostalgic sweet-shop favorite, like extra-thick milk shakes and malteds, towering ice cream sundaes and floats, cherry lime rickeys and orange whips, and of course, the Brooklyn egg cream, perfect for sipping with your sweetheart on a red swivel stool along the bar. Even the hundred-year-old building, which Freeman and Giasullo elected to preserve rather

than renovate, serves as a veritable time machine—think century-old cabinetry stocked with dusty drug and capsule bottles, and an original tiled floor inscribed with the name Lonco's Pharmacy.

First opened as Mrs. Phillip's boarding house in 1884, the building was eventually converted to a pharmacy in the '20s, and taken over a few years later by the owners' son, who peddled pharmaceuticals in front and stolen guns in back. "This old-timer once gave a quote. "Yeah it was a great place. Say some guy was giving you a headache, you could go in there and buy a bottle of aspirin and a .45!" Freeman laughs. Then, after falling into disrepair, the building was briefly inhabited again in the 1990s by the Vermont Market, which carried maple syrup and Christmas trees.

"What's wild is that when they bailed, they left all of their product on the shelves. So when we came in a good thirteen years after that, nothing had changed," Freeman says. "There were remnants of every decade. The only thing there wasn't was anything from the 2000s, so it was kind of spooky. It was like a freeze frame of pharmaceutical history. Of Brooklyn history."

# Sundae of Broken Dreams

(MAKES 1 SUNDAE)

Owner's Note: This sundae has remained on our menu ever since its debut, and was named by *Time Out New York* and *New York magazine* as one of NY's Top Summer Treats in 2011.

½ cup broken pretzel bits (about 3 pretzel rods), in
    pieces no longer than 1-inch long
⅜ cup caramel sauce
2 tennis ball–size scoops of vanilla ice cream
Fresh whipped cream
Whole pretzel rod for garnish (optional)

Put pretzel bits in the bottom of a bowl. Drench with most of the caramel sauce, setting a small amount aside. Place two scoops of ice cream one on top of the other, or side by side, on top of the pretzels. Drizzle remaining caramel sauce over ice cream. Garnish with fresh whipped cream and a whole pretzel rod.

# Butterbeer Egg Cream

(SERVES 1)

Owner's Note: Since the egg cream is only four ingredients deep, it means finding the best milk, filtering the seltzer water so there's less sediment, keeping everything super cold, and serving out of a solid thick glass. And if you're going to make a Brooklyn egg cream, you have to use Fox's U-Bet syrup. If you're going to just make an egg cream, you can do whatever the hell you want.

¼ cup whipped cream
1½ ounces warm caramel sauce
Approximately 1½ cups steamed milk
Approximately ½ cup seltzer

Fill a 12-ounce glass with fresh whipped cream. Pour in warm caramel sauce.

Add steamed, frothy whole milk to the glass until about ½ inch below glass top. Stir contents with an iced-tea spoon. Add seltzer until glass is full. Enjoy!

# BUTTERMILK CHANNEL

524 COURT STREET, CARROLL GARDENS
(718) 852-8490
BUTTERMILKCHANNELNYC.COM
CHEF: RYAN ANGULO

There are two conflicting legends as to how Buttermilk Channel—an old waterway connecting Brooklyn to Governor's Island—got its name. Some say it's because it was shallow enough for cows to be led across during low tide. Others say that the water was actually so rough, it turned the cream carried by travelling dairymen into butter. Either way, it's currently the moniker of a beloved Carroll Gardens bistro, more closely associated with leisurely brunches and addictive duck meatloaf than it is with ancient maritime history.

"Buttermilk Channel is such a unique name with a great story behind it, and it really stuck in our heads," says chef Ryan Angulo. "It's also a singularly Brooklyn name, and when it came down to it, we were really looking to open a restaurant that was dictated by the needs of the neighborhood."

They ended up with an elegant yet rustic American bistro, serving elevated comfort food classics like Fried Chicken and Cheddar Waffles, Pecan Pie Sundaes, and of course, the aforementioned Duck Meatloaf, which sells upward of 150 plates a week.

"It was supposed to be just an occasional blue-plate special, but we quickly realized it was way too popular to ever get rid of," Angulo remembers. "I was just trying to find a different way to use duck, and at the last minute, I ground it all up, mixed it with ketchup, threw it into a pan and cooked it. It tasted pretty good without me putting any effort into it, so I refined it by taking out the ketchup and adding raisins, onions, and soft herbs like thyme and parsley. Just really simple."

That makes the dish surprisingly easy to re-create at home (minus the fancy chef's plating, of course). But whether you choose to grind your own duck or have the butcher do

it for you, Angulo warns to make sure the skin and the meat are processed separately. "The ratio of meat to skin is 4-1," he advises. "You don't want to add in too much skin because it's so fatty, and that will translate to excess fat on the inside of the meatloaf."

## DUCK MEAT LOAF WITH CREAMY PARSNIP PUREE & CRISPY ONIONS

### (SERVES 4)

*For meat loaf:*

1 pound ground duck meat
4 ounces ground duck skin
½ cup minced onion (cooked)
¼ cup chopped raisins
½ cup bread crumbs
2 tablespoons parsley, chopped
1½ teaspoon salt
1 egg
1 tablespoon chopped thyme

*For creamy parsnip puree:*

1 parsnip, peeled and cut into ½-inch pieces.
2 cups whole milk
2 pieces star anise
Zest of one orange
Salt

*For crispy onions:*

1 onion, cut into ¼-inch slices
1 cup buttermilk
2 cups all-purpose flour
1 tablespoon black pepper
Salt
Oil for frying

To prepare the meat loaf: Preheat oven to 400°F. Mix all ingredients. Portion into four equal-size patties. Sear on medium heat in an ovenproof pan and transfer to the oven for 15–20 minutes.

To prepare the parsnip puree: Combine parsnip, milk, and star anise in a small pot. Make sure parsnip is just covered with milk. Cook parsnip till tender. Strain parsnip, reserving liquid. Remove star anise and transfer parsnip to a blender or food processor. Add orange zest and process till smooth, using as much reserved liquid as needed. Season with salt.

To prepare the onion rings: Separate onions into rings and soak in buttermilk. Mix flour and black pepper together. Remove onions from buttermilk and dredge in flour/pepper mixture. Heat oil to 350°F. Fry onions in batches till golden brown. Drain on paper towels and season with salt.

To serve: Divide puree among four plates and top each with one meatloaf patty and two onion rings.

# Chuko

552 VANDERBILT AVENUE, PROSPECT HEIGHTS
(718) 576-6701
BARCHUKO.COM
OWNERS: JAMISON BLANKENSHIP, DAVID KOON, JAMES SATO

Talk about top ramen. Three former chefs from Manhattan's ultimate Japanese eatery, Morimoto, are the brain trust behind Chuko, an equally exciting (although infinitely more casual) noodle house in Prospect Heights. "We all live in Brooklyn, and craft-style ramen just hadn't caught on here yet," explains Jamison Blankenship of their outer-borough move. "But we had no interest in being in the city, where there's lots of competition and big rents."

"The ramen shop in Japan is like the diner in Brooklyn," he adds. "It's the soul of the neighborhood. Our greatest goal was to be that for our community."

Residents have certainly embraced Chuko, lining the gleaming wood counters to feast on crispy kale salad, salt and pepper chicken wings, and of course, silky bowls of ramen, with a much higher pedigree than everyone's favorite college friend, Cup O' Noodles. "Each broth is long-simmered, using antibiotic- and hormone-free meat," says partner David Koon. "We've even had noodles specially designed for us, a different one for each broth, to ensure maximum chewiness, contrast, and flavor. It may seem unnecessary, but when you only have three things in a bowl, the details really matter."

That's not to say there's no happy medium between Chuko's chef-driven creations and four-for-a-dollar dehydrated packets of Maruchan. "At the end of the day it's soup and noodles; there's nothing avant-garde about ramen," Blankenship insists. "You can make a nice simple stock at home. You can find great vegetables, great noodles, great misos, and great soy sauce. There's tremendous access to wonderful ingredients in Brooklyn, which will allow you to make a really decent bowl at home."

## Vegetarian Ramen

### (SERVES 8)

4 ounces dashi kombu (dried kelp)

4 quarts water

⅓ cup soy oil

1 (½-inch) piece ginger, chopped

1 clove garlic, chopped

1 scallion, chopped

8 ounces white miso

8 servings of ramen noodles

Selection of market vegetables

Wipe any dirt from kombu with a damp towel, being careful not to wipe away any white powdery deposits. Soak kombu in water overnight.

Remove the kombu from the water and cut several slits into the leaf. Return the kombu to the water and bring to a boil.

As soon as the water boils, turn off the heat and let steep until the kombu is soft enough to push your finger through. Remove the kombu to prevent the stock from becoming bitter. Place oil, ginger, garlic, and scallion over high heat (approximately 350°F), and fry until golden brown. Remove from heat and refrigerate overnight. Strain.

Bring dashi stock to a boil, blend in miso and two ounces of the ginger-scallion oil until emulsified. Cook noodles to specified time. Ladle soup into bowls, add noodles, and top with any vegetables you like.

# CLOVER CLUB

210 SMITH STREET, COBBLE HILL
(718) 855-7939
CLOVERCLUBNY.COM
OWNER: JULIE REINER

It's often said that there aren't enough women working in professional kitchens. And the same seems to be true behind the bar. But when it comes to top-of-the-line cocktail chefs, there are few names in the business bigger than Julie Reiner, male or female.

Owner and beverage director of the pre-Prohibition-era Clover Club in Cobble Hill, Reiner is often credited with revitalizing the golden age of the cocktail, making American classics with fresh juices, handcrafted syrups and infusions, and seasonal ingredients.

"Prohibition really killed the craft of mixology. So many of the great bartenders couldn't work, so they went to Europe," explains Reiner. "And then the '50s and '60s were the era of making everything easy; powdered mixers, and not using fresh juice. The US never really recovered from that either."

"Mixology is as American as jazz . . . it was born in this country," Reiner continues. "It was ours, we were really good at it, and we want to be really good at it again."

Reiner has certainly put Brooklyn on the map as a leading cocktail destination, with unique tipples like the Green Giant, made with tarragon and sugar snap peas, and the Boathouse Punch, an ode to Brooklyn in a bowl (it's made with local gin and named after the boathouse in Prospect Park.) "Punches are something we've done from the start, because they're communal," says Reiner. "Rather than everybody having a separate experience taste-wise, they just gather around the bowl and drink until it's gone."

And although it's hard to rival the experience of sipping punch at the sexy, sultry Clover Club, Reiner insists the drink is just as easy to re-create at home. "I think it's so interesting that people are willing to make coq au vin, but juicing a lime is just too much," she laughs. "Enjoying a cocktail in the comfort of your own home is great. I do it all the time. I have a four-year-old, which means I don't get out that much anymore!"

## BOATHOUSE PUNCH

(MAKES 20–25 DRINKS)

**Peels of 4 lemons**
**½ cup superfine sugar**
**4½ cups Dorothy Parker gin**
**3 cups Aperol**
**1½ cups St-Germain**
**1½ cups lemon juice**
**1½ cups orange juice**
**1½ cups grapefruit juice**
**1 bottle rosé Champagne**
**Orange wheels, for garnish**

Muddle the lemon peels in ½ cup superfine sugar and let sit for 2 hours. Add the remaining ingredients to a large container and stir. Remove the lemon peels and serve in individual glasses over ice. Garnish with orange wheels.

## GREEN GIANT

(MAKES 1 DRINK)

Owner's Note: This drink was actually created by our wonderful head bartender, Tom Macy.

**4 sugar snap peas, halved, plus two whole snap**
**    peas for garnish**
**8–10 fresh tarragon leaves**
**¾ ounce simple syrup**
**2 ounces Hayman's Old Tom gin**
**¾ ounce lemon juice**
**½ ounce dry vermouth**
**Crushed ice**

Muddle 4 halved sugar snap peas and 8–10 tarragon leaves in simple syrup. Add remaining ingredients. Shake and strain into rocks glass over crushed ice, and garnish with two snap peas.

Note: The drink can also be adapted beautifully with London Dry gin, in which case omit the dry vermouth.

# A Brooklyn Cocktail Guide

Remember the days when you just walked into a bar and ordered a beer (with little to no thought of craft ales or microbrews), or watered-down well drinks, like rum and cokes, vodka tonics, seabreezes, and screwdrivers? Neither do we. It seems like almost every bar nowadays has a dedicated mixologist, patiently shaking, stirring, infusing, and muddling a seemingly endless variety of Prohibition-era cocktails. Can't tell your juleps and smashes from your collins and fizzes, or your fixes and sours from your punches and royales? Next time you're looking to have a nightcap in Brooklyn, don't leave the house without our handy dandy guide!

**Fixes and Daisies:** A spirit of any kind with citrus, a cordial, and carbonated water added.

**Slings and Toddies:** A spirit of any kind with water, sugar, and spice added. Served hot or cold.

**Cups and Cobblers:** Wine or beer of any kind with fruit, herbs, sugar, and carbonated water added.

**Sours and Fizzes:** A spirit of any kind with citrus and a sweetener added. Can be served with or without an egg white and/or carbonated water.

**Juleps and Smashes:** A spirit of any kind with sugar and mint added. Can be served with or without citrus.

**Flips, Possets, and Nogs:** A spirit of any kind, with sugar, spice, and dairy added. Served hot or cold.

# COLONIE

127 ATLANTIC AVENUE, BROOKLYN HEIGHTS
(718) 855-7500
COLONIENYC.COM
OWNERS: EMELIE KIHLSTROM, ELISE ROSENBERG, TAMER HAMAWI
CHEF: BRYAN REDMOND

Before Colonie joined Kickstarter in 2010, the crowd-funding site was used mostly to finance short indie films and demo albums. But when the restaurant ended up exceeding its $15,000 goal (which went toward a countertop, kitchen appliances, tiled walls, and pendant lamps), Kickstarter—and Colonie—quickly became the talk of the culinary world.

"They rejected us at first because they didn't see restaurants as being a creative art form," remembers co-owner Emelie Kihlstrom. "We wrote a passionate appeal explaining the art involved in the restaurant industry, from the design to the food to the theatrics of the open kitchen. We won them over, and now it seems every other young food business is on Kickstarter, which is amazing!"

And monetary benefits aside, the restaurateurs insist that the most valuable advantage of using Kickstarter was the rapport they built with the community. Literally having had a hand in helping them open, the neighborhood tracked their build-out with an added sense of anticipation, and have taken an almost proprietary pleasure in their continued success.

"When we opened in Brooklyn Heights and then DUMBO, there weren't a ton of great restaurants yet. So we've been inspired on a daily basis by residents who are so excited to have us in their hood," says co-owner Elise Rosenberg. "They actually thanked us for opening! That gives us tremendous motivation to keep the locals happy, and gets us especially excited by what we're doing."

# CARROT SALAD

(SERVES 4)

1 pound baby carrots
Extra-virgin olive oil, for drizzling
Salt and pepper to taste
2 heads garlic
1 bunch thyme
8 ounces Greek yogurt
Zest and juice of 1 orange
1 cup sunflower seeds
1 cup sunflower oil
Canola oil, for frying
1 cup confectioners' sugar
Sunflower shoots, for garnish

Preheat oven to 400°F.

Toss the carrots with olive oil, salt, and pepper, garlic heads, and thyme, and place on a baking sheet. Roast for about 45 minutes, or until tender.

In a mixing bowl, combine the yogurt and the orange juice and zest. Season with a pinch of salt.

Heat oven to 350°F. Toast sunflower seeds in oven for about 15 minutes or until golden brown. Remove to a bowl, and cover in sunflower oil.

Heat a pot of canola oil to 275°F. Peel and roughly chop one of the heads of roasted garlic. Toss in confectioners' sugar and add to the oil. Fry until golden brown, stirring almost constantly. Strain and cool.

To plate, toss cooled, roasted carrots with the sunflower seeds and sunflower oil, candied garlic, and salt and pepper to taste. Arrange on a plate with a few dollops of the orange yogurt. Garnish with sunflower shoots.

# Do or Dine

1108 Bedford Avenue, Bedford Stuyvesant
(718) 684-2290
doordinebk.com
Owners: Justin Warner and George McNeese

The Bed Stuy eatery Do or Dine is undeniably quirky. Think menu staples like foie gras–filled doughnuts and Nippon Nachos (fried gyoza topped with melted cheese and sour cream), and in lieu of standard signage, their name emblazoned on the underside of a West Indian bakery awning. "It's just that we couldn't afford to change it," laughs co-owner Justin Warner. "Our other rationale was that the sign has been here more than ten years, and the space has been vacant for six. So if we put a sign up and the restaurant closes, the same thing is going to happen. So, we're kind of like hermit crabs, you know what I mean?"

So how did a group of guys from the exclusive Manhattan restaurant The Modern wind up serving (as it's often been described), "haute stoner food" in Bed Stuy, anyway? "We all lived out here already," Warner explains. "So after work, we would just dump a bunch of money in the Midtown economy, pay for cabs, and come back and have no money. We figured we were either an accurate sample or a total anomaly, but hoped that people in a similar bind would come here and put money back into the community."

The grand plan definitely seems to have worked. Now that everyone knows to peep under the West Indian sign, Do or Dine has become a haven for neighborhood night owls and adventurous foodies alike. And although oddball creations like Pond Wings (Dr Pepper–glazed frog's legs) and E666's (deviled eggs) continue to get most of the attention, Warner insists the tame sounding cumin lamb breast is Do or Dine's signature dish. "It's the first thing George and I ever made together. We were broke as a joke

when we moved to Brooklyn, and lamb breast is relatively cheap per pound," Warner remembers. "We experimented with cooking it all sorts of ways and it was horrible; really chewy and rough. Then one day, we put it in the oven and started playing video games and forgot it was in there. And four hours later we're like, whoa, something smells really good!"

"That's kind of what we're about," he adds. "Stuff that makes you happy and makes you smile inside a little, but something that's not too much labor. Labor sucks."

# CUMIN LAMB BREAST

(SERVES 1)

¼ cup cumin seeds
¼ cup kosher salt
¼ cup whole black peppercorns
⅛ cup coriander seeds
1 bone-in lamb breast

Grind up all of the spices in a blender or spice grinder. This is your rub.

Flip the lamb breast over so that the bony side is up. Use a sharp knife to remove all of the transparent gristly stuff from above and around the bones. Leave the bones in for now.

Hit the breast with the rub and then roast on a roasting rack with a pan to catch *a lot* of drippings at 225°F–250°F for 6–8 hours, depending on your oven. It's not really a science, because we're going to cook it again when we serve it.

Remove from the oven. Allow it to cool completely. Remove the big rib bones. They should pop right out.

Slice into 8–10 pieces. You may have to cut through some cartilage but don't fear.

When you are ready to serve, reheat the lamb pieces until warm, ideally in a 400°F oven for 8–10 minutes. You could also do it in a pan or on a grill.

# DU JOUR BAKERY

365 5TH AVENUE, PARK SLOPE
(347) 227-8953
DUJOURBAKERY.COM
OWNERS: TJ AND VERA OBIAS

The name may be Du Jour, but Park's Slope's newest bakery doesn't peddle in trends. Instead, the sweet shop's straightforward mission statement is to turn out carby, sugary basics really, really well (everything, including the croissants, is made in-house daily). "Opening in Park Slope was an obvious choice for us, because our target audience is really kid- and family-friendly," says TJ Obias, who runs the shop with his wife, Vera. "Park Slope has kids, families, young people, commuters . . . I guess that's what drew us to the neighborhood."

It also doesn't hurt that the bakery is literally fifty-five paces away from their own apartment (they counted), which is a welcome change from all the years they spent trekking back and forth from Manhattan (he at restaurants like Morimoto and Cafe Gray, she at the Russian Tea Room and Dovetail). "I would see the people that I worked with more than I got to see my wife, and after a year that really wears on you," TJ says. "The days are hard here, don't get me wrong. But now I don't have to wonder what Vera's doing, because she's right next to me or she's downstairs."

To be specific, she's probably whipping up batches of the shop's signature bread pudding, which was downsized from a three-star restaurant dessert to the decadent, handheld pastry it's become. "Don't be afraid to make the recipe from scratch; that's part of the fun. Although the idea of baking bread was always a scary thing for me too," Vera concedes. "So if you really need to buy it, just come here and get it!"

# ALMOND BREAD PUDDING

(MAKES 20)

*For the frangipane (makes 1 quart):*

4 ounces (1 stick) unsalted butter

½ cup sugar

5 eggs

½ cup almond flour

3 tablespoons pastry flour

*For the maple butter sauce:*

4 ounces (1 stick) unsalted butter

½ cup light brown sugar

1 cup maple syrup

1 cup heavy cream

1 teaspoon salt

1 teaspoon vanilla extract

*For the bread pudding:*

1½ loaves brioche

3 cups milk

3 cups heavy cream

5 eggs

5 egg yolks

2 teaspoons vanilla extract

¾ cup sugar

*To finish:*

Extra sugar for sprinkling

Sliced almonds for sprinkling

To make the frangipane: In a stand mixer with the paddle attachment, cream together the butter and sugar. Add the eggs one by one and mix until mixture is uniform. Add almond flour and pastry flour and mix until just combined.

To make the maple butter sauce: Brown the butter in a saucepot then add sugar, syrup, and cream. Bring to a simmer and strain. Add the salt and vanilla.

To make the bread pudding: Cut brioche to 1-inch cubes and set aside. In a bowl, combine the rest of the ingredients and strain. Add to brioche and allow to soak in refrigerator overnight. Using a spider, extract bread out of custard mixture and fill 5-ounce baking cups. Spread evenly with frangipane and sprinkle with sugar and sliced almonds. Bake at 350°F for 20–25 minutes or until custard is set. Top with maple butter sauce and serve warm.

# EGG

135 NORTH 5TH STREET, WILLIAMSBURG
(718) 302-5151
PIGANDEGG.COM
OWNER: GEORGE WELD

George Weld is one of Brooklyn's leading sustainability advocates. He sources from human-scale purveyors, putting more than $200,000 per year into the pockets of small and organic producers. He offers fair pay and benefits to his employees, and the opportunity to work with food from beginning to end, starting with the produce grown at his small, self-supplying farm upstate. And through his involvement with organizations like Slow Money (which funds ventures that contribute to the building of more efficient, locally based food systems), he's encouraging like-minded restaurants to do the same.

So how did he become known as the king of Brooklyn brunch?

"Eggs are one of nature's prime examples of when the real version is so much better than the factory farm version," explains Weld. "You can't always taste a dramatic difference between organic, earth-bound lettuce and generic, conventional lettuce. But

since eggs absorb the chicken's feed so totally, they can really change over the course of the year based on what the chickens are doing. So they're one of those things that, in their simplicity, are still really revelatory."

That means, the all-day breakfast at Weld's Williamsburg eatery is a meal you can feel really good about—ethically and otherwise. You can order farm-fresh eggs until 6 p.m., either paired with organic grits, in an omelet with Grafton cheddar and broiled tomatoes, or served alongside insanely tasty buttermilk biscuits.

So does Weld agree that the mark of a highly skilled chef is his or her ability to properly cook an egg?

"There's really nowhere to hide with eggs. Once you mess them up, there's no way to fudge it," he affirms. "So you have to pay attention and learn to watch for different things, like the way that the inner white sets, or how hot the pan is when you drop the egg in." He shakes his head and grins. "For something so seemingly basic, eggs definitely keep you on your toes."

# SOURED-MILK BISCUITS

### (MAKES 36 BISCUITS)

Owner's Note: Since Brooklyn is such a bagel town, biscuits are a real stand-apart item on our menu. They're delicious and simple and everyone finds a different way of getting them right. They tend to take on a different character depending on who's making them, which is kind of how the kitchen here runs, generally!

4 pounds and 14 ounces flour (half unbleached,
   all-purpose flour and half cake flour)
½ cup plus 1 tablespoon baking powder
4 tablespoons salt
3 tablespoons sugar
8 ounces butter, cut into cubes and put in the freezer
7½ cups buttermilk/soured milk*
10 ounces butter, sliced into thin sheets and
   put in the freezer

Keep all ingredients cold and dry throughout.

* To make sour milk, add ½ cup of cider vinegar to 7 cups of milk and stir.

Preheat oven to 500°F. In a large bowl, sift together flour, baking powder, salt and sugar. Blend cubed butter into flour mix with your hands. Work quickly and cut butter in until flour resembles very coarse meal with a few pea-size lumps. Add *most* of the milk (reserve around ½ cup until you see how the dough coheres and add if necessary) to flour and butter. *Work quickly.*

Mix milk in with a rubber spatula, mixing only until the dough begins to hold together. Dump dough onto floured work surface and pat into a rough rectangle about ½-inch thick. Use a bench scraper to ensure dough isn't sticking to table. Layer the sheets of frozen butter across the dough and fold the whole thing up in three folds across. Gently pat down again to ¾ inch and cut out some biscuits. Don't stretch or knead the dough.

Use a 2½-inch biscuit cutter to cut biscuits from dough. Do *not* twist cutter. Space biscuits ½ inch apart onto well-buttered half sheet pan. Brush tops with leftover sour milk. Bake for 13–18 minutes. Biscuits should be well-risen and light; if they feel wet or heavy, bake them longer.

# ELBERTA

335 Flatbush Avenue, Prospect Heights
(718) 638-1936
ELBERTARESTAURANT.COM
Owners: Erwin Caesar and Erica Philips

Right on the main drag of Flatbush Avenue, elberta is within coveted proximity to the new Barclay's Center. And whatever your opinion is on the giant sports complex, it's proven to be a boon for many of the restaurants around it—a chance to draw in dinner crowds on their way to a Nets game or Jay-Z concert. Not that elberta doesn't have what it takes to be a great go-to spot for locals.

The restaurant is a first-time venture for owners Erwin Caesar and wife Erica Philips, both of whom have managed to maintain their day jobs (he's an IT consultant, and she's in healthcare). "We pretty much see each other in passing," Philips admits, laughing. And to be sure, the intimate eatery has undergone a few growing pains in the last couple of years, changing chefs and flirting with a Southern-inspired menu that's been gradually phased out. But after realizing that there's no straight path to success in an increasingly competitive market, the restaurateurs have finally come into their own.

"We realized that, even though we may not have had the background, we have to trust that we know why we went into this and what we want to accomplish," says Philips. "We wanted to represent the diversity of the neighborhood we're in, as well as the diversity of our Caribbean backgrounds. We're really trying to be true to ourselves now, by wrapping our own flavors into the cuisine."

# GOAT RAVIOLI

(SERVES 8)

*For the braised goat:*

10 pounds goat neck

1 cup vegetable or canola oil

2 ounces fresh ginger, peeled and sliced

2 onions, sliced

½ bunch thyme

1 cup Madras curry powder

3 tablespoons turmeric

2 gallons goat stock (can substitute beef stock)

*For the pasta dough:*

3 cups all-purpose flour

2 large eggs

3 tablespoons water

1 teaspoon olive oil

½ teaspoon salt

*For the cauliflower puree:*

1 head cauliflower

2 quarts heavy cream

1 cup Parmesan cheese

*For the pickled raisins:*

1 cup golden raisins

2 cups rice vinegar

½ cup sugar

½ cup allspice berries

*For the turnips:*

2 cups baby white turnips, peeled

2 tablespoons butter

To make the braised goat: Sear goat neck in a large, ovenproof stock pot with oil covering the bottom. Once all sides are seared, take the goat neck out and reserve. Add the ginger, onions, and thyme to the pot and sauté. Toast the curry powder and turmeric in a pan, then add it to the onions and ginger. Place the goat neck back in the pot and add the goat stock. Cover loosely with tin foil, and place in oven at 300°F. Cook until tender, about 3 hours. Let cool, and with two forks or your fingers, remove the meat from the bones. Set aside.

To make the pasta: Make a well with the flour on a flat surface. In a measuring cup, mix the eggs, water, oil, and salt. Pour the wet mixture slowly into the flour and mix with two fingers until all of the wet is incorporated. Do not force the dough to take all of the flour. Form dough into a disk and cover with plastic wrap. Place in the refrigerator for 2 hours to rest. Pass through a pasta machine to make thin layers.

To make the cauliflower puree: Cut up cauliflower and cook in the heavy cream until tender. Once cauliflower is cooked, drain through a colander but save the cream. Puree the cauliflower in a blender with a little bit of the cream and cheese.

For the pickled raisins: Combine raisins, vinegar, sugar, and allspice in a pot, set over medium heat. Bring to a simmer, and cook until raisins are plump, about 5 minutes.

For the turnips: Blanch turnips in salted boiling water for 2 minutes. Toss with butter.

To make the ravioli: Arrange tablespoon-size dollops of the braised goat 1½ inches apart on each one of the pasta sheets. Brush a little egg white around each dollop, then place another sheet directly on top. Gently press around the filling to remove any air pockets and seal the sheets. Using a ravioli or cookie cutter, cut each

of the ravioli into circles. Crimp the edges by pressing down on the dough with the tines of a fork. Sprinkle with flour to prevent the dough from sticking. Cook the ravioli in plenty of boiling salted water until they float to the top, 3–4 minutes. Drain well. Plate ravioli with the cauliflower puree, pickled raisins, and blanched turnips.

# Winter White Pear Sangria

### (MAKES 6 DRINKS)

*For the herb-infused sangria:*

1 stalk lemon grass, pounded with the flat of a knife to release juices

2 sprigs of thyme

2 sage leaves

4 sprigs of parsley

6 basil leaves

6 mint leaves

1 bottle of sweet wine, like Moscato or Riesling

½ cup pineapple juice

½ cup fruit puree, like peach, mango, pear, or plum

½ cup fruit brandy, like apricot, apple, or pear

½ cup peach schnapps

*For the cocktails:*

Lime juice, for rimming

Dried citrus zest, for rimming

Turbinado sugar, for rimming

Herb-infused sangria

6 spoonfuls of fresh mixed fruit

Champagne, for topping off

To make the sangria: Muddle cleaned herbs in a glass container. Add in all of the liquid, and seal the container. Allow to sit for a few days—the longer it sits, the more herbaceous the sangria will be. Mix and strain before using.

To make the cocktails: Dip half of the rim of 6 wineglasses in lime juice, and then in a mix of the citrus zest and turbinado sugar. Fill glasses with ice, and add 1 cup of the sangria mix and 1 spoonful of fruit to each. Top off with Champagne.

# FLETCHER'S BROOKLYN BARBECUE

433 3RD AVENUE, GOWANUS
(347) 763-2680
FLETCHERSBKLYN.COM
OWNER: BILLY FLETCHER
PITMASTER: MATT FISHER

As much as we'd like to argue otherwise, Brooklyn's never really been a contender against the great barbecue capitals of America. But add Fletcher's to the ever-increasing roster of estimable pit stops throughout the borough (think Fette Sau, Briskettown, Mable's, Dinosaur, and Fort Reno), and Brooklyn 'cue might just change the course of history. "Barbecue is a religion, so whatever you grow up with is what barbecue means to you," says owner Billy Fletcher. "We're finally seeing real wood cooking around here, with a little more flavor and a little more spice, backed by careful sourcing and quality ingredients that are so integral to Brooklyn's foodie culture. All it's going to take is more local people loving what we make, to really fuel the legitimacy of Northeast barbecue."

It's hard not to appreciate the meat from Joanie—the name of their red oak and sugar maple–burning smoker. In addition to classics like St. Louis–style ribs, juicy brisket, fiery hot links, and melt-in-your mouth burnt ends, Fletcher's has become known for using unusual cuts and experimenting with globetrotting flavor combos, like *char siu* or coriander pork steak, BBQ lamb, and smoked duck tacos. Even the chicken, so often a dry, sad afterthought for the red meat–adverse, is a triumph. Unfailingly tender and uncommonly flavorful, it's even better when dipped in a creamy pool of Brooklyn White Sauce. "White barbecue sauce is most commonly found in Alabama, and historically made with mayo, lemon juice, vinegar, cayenne, and black pepper . . . pretty simple and straight up," Fisher explains. "But we spiked it with a little horseradish, a variety of chiles, and some fresh herbs, like dill and chives. It's a little more upscale and spicy but not dirty, which makes it all the more New York."

# Barbecue Chicken with Brooklyn White Sauce

(SERVES 4–6)

1 3½ pound chicken

*For the rub:*

1 tablespoon kosher salt
1 tablespoon fresh-cracked black pepper
2 teaspoons granulated garlic
1 teaspoon light brown sugar
1 teaspoon chile powder
1 disposable aluminum pan
4 cups water
2 wood chunks: 1 chunk of oak plus 1 chunk of maple.
　 If maple and oak are not available, use hickory.

*For the Brooklyn White Sauce:*

1 cup mayonnaise
½ cup cider vinegar
1 tablespoon white prepared horseradish
1 tablespoon fresh lemon juice
1 tablespoon kosher salt
½ teaspoon black pepper
½ tablespoon minced fresh chives
¼ teaspoon minced fresh dill
½ teaspoon ground cayenne pepper
1 teaspoon granulated sugar

*Special equipment:*

Hardwood lump charcoal

In a small bowl, combine kosher salt, black pepper, garlic, brown sugar, and chili powder to make the rub. Remove the chicken from the refrigerator, season the chicken inside and out with the rub and set it aside.

Light one full charcoal chimney of hardwood lump charcoal. While the chimney heats, place the disposable pan in the bottom of the grill on the side opposite the air vents. Fill the pan with the water. When the flames are nearly reaching the top of the chimney, dump coals in the empty side of the grill. Using tongs, carefully wedge the chunks of wood into the charcoal. As soon as you see wisps of smoke, place the cooking grid in place and cover the grill. Ensure the bottom vents are all the way open and preheat the grill for 5 minutes.

Remove the lid, brush the cooking grate to ensure it is clean, and place the chicken on the grate above the water pan. Return the lid with the air vents positioned above the chicken. Set the vents in the grill lid to half open.

After 30 minutes, remove the lid, and rotate the chicken 180 degrees. Cover the grill and continue cooking until the chicken registers 170°F on a thermometer inserted between the leg and thigh, roughly 30–40 more minutes.

Remove the chicken to a platter, loosely tent with foil and let it rest 15 minutes. In a bowl, combine all the ingredients for the white sauce and whisk well to ensure the sugar dissolves completely. Carve chicken and serve with Brooklyn White Sauce.

Leftover chicken makes a wonderful sandwich. Warm the chicken, then carefully pull all the meat away from the bones. Discard the skin, bones and cartilage and serve the meat on a fluffy sandwich roll with a healthy dose of Brooklyn White Sauce.

# Fort Defiance

365 Van Brunt Street, Red Hook
(347) 453-6672
FORTDEFIANCEBROOKLYN.COM
Owner: St. John Frizell

Fort Defiance is the perfect place to a get a great cup of coffee, an expertly executed cocktail, or a superb meal in Red Hook, any time of day or night. But it's also part of a larger, sociological thesis. "There's this book by Ray Oldenburg called *The Great Good Place*. He talks about the vital role that informal public gathering spaces, specifically cafes and restaurants, play in American life and all around the globe," explains owner St. John Frizell. "I felt like my community didn't have a lot of those. There are good bars here, but if you're not a real bar-goer or you socialize during the day, there were literally no options. So that was the idea behind Fort Defiance."

And although the devastation of Hurricane Sandy might have signaled the end of Frizell's "great good place" (the entire basement was flooded, the dining room took on a foot of water, and he lost the bulk of his equipment and inventory), it wound up being the greatest argument for his social experiment yet. Two days after the storm, he helped form the group Restore Red Hook, which went on to raise half a million dollars to benefit fifty-five small businesses throughout the neighborhood.

"About half of the money came from big charities like the Robin Hood Foundation, but the only reason we got grants from those big charities was because we were able to do all this groundwork, grassroots fundraising," says Frizell. "And by we, I mean Brooklyn residents donating their own money, and little bars and restaurants all over the borough holding their own one-night fund-raisers for us. It was the community itself that really picked Red Hook up."

## The Pundit

(MAKES 1 DRINK)

*For the coffee-infused scotch:*

1 liter good blended scotch (we use White Horse
   for this)
8 tablespoons whole espresso beans

*For the drink:*

1½ ounces of coffee-infused blended scotch
1½ ounces Cocchi Torino, or any good vermouth
1 teaspoon Amaro dell'Erborista

Combine scotch and espresso beans in a glass
jar. Stir. Wait 8 minutes, stirring occasionally. Pour
through a coffee filter. Stir 1½ ounces of the coffee-
infused scotch with the remaining ingredients over
ice in a mixing glass; strain into a chilled cocktail
glass. Garnish with an orange twist.

## The Dagger

(MAKES 1 DRINK)

The Dagger was created for a cocktail competition held at the premiere of a production of Ver-
di's *Macbeth* at the Metropolitan Opera in 2012.

1½ ounces Hendrick's gin
¾ ounce Cocchi Americano
½ ounce lemon juice
¼ ounce simple syrup
¼ ounce Bittermens Amère Sauvage liqueur (which was
   originally made in Red Hook—Bittermens has since
   moved to New Orleans)

Combine all ingredients and shake over ice.
Strain into a large rocks glass filled with ice.
Garnish with a grapefruit twist.

# Gran Electrica

5 Front Street, DUMBO
(718) 852-2700
GRANELECTRICA.COM
Owners: Tamer Hamawi, Emelie Kihlstrom, Elise Rosenberg

Gran Electrica is so determinedly funky that the food is almost an added benefit. Located in an oversize space on Front Street—formerly the oldest office building in Brooklyn—the Mexican restaurant has serious eye appeal. In fact, you could spend the better part of the day poring over the custom-designed Day of the Dead wallpaper, which features skeletons frolicking in classic, Brooklyn Heights–inspired tableaus. Like subjects of a borough-centric Where's Waldo, you'll find them cavorting on the carousel, walking dogs across the bridge, taking wedding pictures by the pier, and pushing strollers and riding scooters down the cobblestone streets.

Of course, market-inspired dishes like peekytoe crab tostadas, oyster mushroom quesadillas, and citrus-marinated carne asada are pretty great too—especially when

accompanied by one of the tequila or mezcal-based cocktails devised by co-owner Tamer Hamawi.

"A lot of places use frozen purees or juices. We juice our beets, carrots, grapefruits, cukes, or whatever we are using in our seasonal drinks on a daily basis," Hamawi says. "If you honor the ingredients, it's pretty hard to mess up."

So what are some of his other fail-safe tips for making quality cocktails at home?"

"You'll need a cocktail shaker, a Hawthorne strainer, a measuring jigger, a stirring bar spoon, and good ice," Hamawi advises. "And only buy the best spirits and use fresh juices. It's that simple!"

## MARGARITA DE REMOLACHA

(SERVES 1)

Lime juice and lime salt for rimming
1½ ounces Pueblo Viejo blanco tequila
   (or any 100% blue agave)
½ ounce Combier liqueur or other triple sec
1 ounce fresh beet juice
1 ounce fresh lime juice
½ ounce simple syrup
Ice
Sliced fresh beet and a wheel of lime,
   for garnish

Prepare a rocks glass by rimming the glass with lime juice and then dipping into lime salt (sea salt combined with lime zest). In a large cocktail shaker, combine next 5 ingredients with 1 cup of ice. Shake vigorously and strain over fresh ice cubes in prepared rocks glass. Garnish with a skewered thinly sliced fresh beet and a lime wheel.

# NEIL GANIC: BROOKLYN'S BEST CHARACTER

Every town has its characters. Often lovable, wholly idiosyncratic, and just plain eccentric, they become part of the unique identity of the neighborhood in which they live. One of our very favorite restaurant characters currently presides over an equally quirky community, The Columbia Waterfront District, a cobblestoned parcel of land snaking toward Red Hook, in the shadow of the BQE. His name is Neil Ganic, owner of Petite Crevette, a catch-of-the-day seafood restaurant that has remained BYOB, website free (they also rarely pick up the phone), and cash-only, since opening in 2007. "He just hangs out in a fedora and listens to Cuban music all afternoon, waiting on customers to come in for lunch," laughs our photographer, Eric. And come they do . . . the famously irascible Ganic has become known for his antics as much as for his pristine, fresher-than-fresh food. Take the time he charged out of the kitchen and hurled a live lobster at a pair of patrons after they complained about the underdone specimen in their cioppino, and then banned them from the restaurant for life. "I didn't throw it," Ganic amends. "I walked downstairs and picked the biggest daddy from the seaweed and left it in the middle of the table. Is this fresh enough for you?" You know what else a true character does? He opens a watering hole right next to the restaurant two years later called, what else? The Flying Lobster bar. Only in Brooklyn, my friends. Only in Brooklyn. Petite Crevette is located at 144 Union Street (718-855-2632).

# Hawker Bar

611 Vanderbilt Avenue, Prospect Heights
(347) 915-1000
HAWKERBARNYC.COM
Owner: Heathe St. Clair

Hawker Bar, a down-under eatery in the heart of Prospect Heights, wants to teach you how to really speak Australian. So don't expect Vegemite, fish-and-chips, or shrimp on the barbie. "The restaurant represents what I grew up eating in Australia, which was partly meat pies and fried seafood, sure, but largely Southeast Asian cuisine," said owner Heathe St. Clair.

"The truth is, Australian food doesn't really exist," he added. "It's a jumble of influences from all of the countries that surround it, flavors brought in by great chefs passing through."

Hawker Bar pays particular homage to the street food peddled by vendors throughout Australia, like Chinese steam buns, Indonesian satay, Thai summer rolls, Indian curry, and the popular Wrap and Roll—a selection of savory fillings like short ribs, shiso shrimp, crispy tofu, and braised pork belly, served with roti, lettuce cups, and an assortment of pickled vegetables and fresh herbs.

"I like the idea of eating with my hands, trying different things, and making my own flavors," says St. Clair. "But the best part of the dish is that it's communal. I really love being able to interact and share a dining experience with others."

# "WRAP AND ROLL" ROTI & LETTUCE CUPS

### (SERVES 2–4)

Note: There are no rules when it comes to constructing these—just place your desired fillings inside the roti or lettuce leaves, top with your choice of sauce, guacamole, pickled vegetables and/or fresh herbs, and enjoy!

*To serve:*

Packaged roti (a Southeast Asian flatbread)
Boston, bibb, or butter lettuce leaves
Roti sauce (can be found at Asian or West Indian
   grocery stores; or substitute any chile sauce)
Guacamole
Pickled carrots and daikon
Fresh basil, mint, and cilantro leaves
Prepared filling (Thai Crispy Chicken and/or Salt and
   Pepper Squid, recipes below)

*For the Thai Crispy Chicken filling:*

2 boneless chicken thighs
2 cups yellow curry paste
2 tablespoons curry powder
1 tablespoon palm sugar
2 tablespoons fish sauce
1 tablespoon salt
3 tablespoons oil, plus extra for frying
1 tablespoon sugar
1 (13.5-ounce) can coconut milk

Preheat oven to 375°F. Whisk all marinade ingredients together until smooth and add the chicken. Let marinate for at least an hour. Oil a grill or griddle pan and cook chicken skin side down for 2 minutes, then flip and cook on the other side for 2 minutes. Transfer to hot plate and finish in oven for 2–3 minutes until fully cooked. Cut evenly into ¼-inch strips.

*For the Salt & Pepper Squid filling:*

For the five-spice mix:

1 tablespoon ground ginger
1 tablespoon celery powder
1 tablespoon chicken stock powder
1 tablespoon salt
1 teaspoon five-spice powder

For the squid:

½ pound fresh whole squid
3 tablespoons self-rising flour
Vegetable oil
Rice flour
2 spring onions, chopped
1 garlic clove, chopped
½ Thai red chile, chopped
1 tablespoon rice wine

Combine the ingredients for the five-spice mix and set aside. Clean the squid by pulling the tentacles from the body. Wash out the tube and remove the clear "backbone." Peel off the skin if desired. Cut the tentacles from the head and discard the head. Cut the tube into triangles, which helps the squid to curl during cooking.

In a bowl, mix the self-rising flour with 1 tablespoon of vegetable oil and a little water to make a paste. Add the squid pieces and tentacles and coat well. Sprinkle and toss with enough rice flour until the pieces are dry. Heat enough vegetable oil in a wok for deep-frying. Add the

squid in batches and cook until golden and crisp. Remove with a wire basket or slotted spoon. When all the squid is cooked, drain most of the oil from the wok. Add the spring onions, garlic, and chile to the wok. Stir-fry for 20 seconds, until aromatic. Return the squid to the wok, add 1–1½ teaspoons of five-spice mix and toss well. Add the rice wine, toss and serve right away.

# Mr. Lee's Mystical 1-Inch Punch

### (MAKES 2 COCKTAILS)

"Fosters" may be Australian for beer. But when it comes to cocktails at Hawker Bar, "Mr. Lee's Mystical 1-Inch Punch" is Brooklynese for simply delicious. A blend of three different rums, pineapple juice, masala agave, and ginseng, the smoky concoction is just one of mixologist Greg Seider's intoxicating Australasian libations. "I've always been influenced by Asian flavors, like Thai, Indian, and Vietnamese," says Seider. "And all of my cocktail inspiration comes from cooking. When I cook—and eat—ideas for flavors mix around in my head." Can't hightail it over to Hawker Bar for a taste? Get shaking at home with this creative cocktail recipe.

2 ounces Diplomatico rum
2 ounces Denizen rum
1 ounce Goslings rum
2 ounces pineapple juice
1½ ounces masala agave
1 ounce lemon juice
1 ounce lime juice
1 ounce water
10 drops ginseng
Approximately 1 cup Ginger beer

Shake first 9 ingredients over ice and strain into a teapot. Top with ginger beer.

# L&B Spumoni Gardens

2725 86th Street, Gravesend
(718) 449-1230
SPUMONIGARDENS.COM
Chef and Co-owner: Lenny Kern

Dishes begin to pile up on our table. Sausage and veggie–studded pasta crowned with a runny fried egg, and fat, fried shrimp glazed with Marsala wine and Calabrian fig molasses. Rosemary-scented veal chops strewn with shiitake mushrooms and apples, and an intricately stacked pyramid of caramelized lemons and sole. Patrons look up quizzically from their baked ziti, rice balls, and chicken parmigiana. Are we visiting celebrities? Bosom buddies with the owners? Well, that certainly never hurts, but no. "We keep our traditional menu, but if you know better, you ask for the Chef's Table," says Lenny Kern, longtime chef and co-owner of Gravesend's iconic L&B Spumoni Gardens. "I'll just send out whatever's best in the market that day. Fresh, seasonal variations of classic dishes. Even the old-timers go for it on occasion."

"I think me seeing an old-school Italian trying something that I made new-school is the greatest thing in the world," he adds. "Because it's hard to get them to change their stripes."

Not that Kern's some upstart young gun looking to reinvent the wheel. He's been working at the pizzeria since he was a teenager, eventually marrying Camille Barbati (descendant of original owner, Ludovico, who famously peddled his wares from a horse and wagon, before setting up shop on 86th Street in 1939). Kern has just never been content to ride on a wave of nostalgia, preferring to constantly improve, update, and look forward, starting with the adjunct restaurant he helped open in 1973. "You know that song, you got to be in with the in-crowd? I think Brooklyn's the new in-crowd. There's a freedom to be different, to be radical, that Manhattan has never had," Kern proclaims. "I look at the restaurant business as an artistic endeavor. When all you're thinking about is money and profit margins, it puts you at a disadvantage."

But for all of Kern's creativity and risk-taking, what about the people who just can't separate L&B from its legendary squares and spumoni? "Let them order pizza," Kern says, waving a hand dismissively. "I call the takeout window our slot machine . . . ka-ching, ka-ching! Because whatever money they make from that, I put right back into the restaurant."

"You see that pie over there?" he asks, gesturing into the courtyard. "It just bought me the next size up of shrimp."

## PISAN FARMHOUSE PASTA

(SERVES 4, OR 2 L&B-STYLE)

*For the sausage:*

4 links Italian sausage (2 hot and 2 sweet)
2 cups chicken stock
1 (28-ounce) can plum tomatoes
2 cloves roasted garlic
1 bunch fresh basil
½ cup plus 1 shot white wine

*For the sauce:*

2 tablespoons extra-virgin olive oil
1 quart good tomato sauce
1 skinless Sicilian eggplant, cut into cubes and roasted
½ pound veal scaloppine, thinly sliced and grilled
½ cup fresh peas

*For the pasta:*

1 pound dried pasta, like bucatini, cooked
    according to package directions
1 whole raw egg plus 4 fried eggs
Grated Grana Padano, to serve

To make the sausage: Place sausages in a roasting pan. Cook in a 500°F oven for 35 minutes. Remove from oven and fill the pan ½-inch higher than the sausages with chicken stock, plum tomatoes, roasted garlic, basil, and ½ cup white wine. Cover with foil. Reduce the oven to 350°F and add the sausages. Cook for 1½ hours. Remove, and cut sausage into 1-inch chunks.

To finish: Add olive oil to the bottom of a large pot, followed by the tomato sauce and the shot of white wine. Add roasted eggplant, veal, sausage, and peas. Add pasta to sauce. Add 6 whole leaves of fresh basil, and as you finish stirring, the whole raw egg. Serve topped with Grana Padano and the fried eggs.

# Dueling Pork Chops

(SERVES 2)

1 center-cut pork chop, pounded very thin
Canola oil
1 sprig fresh rosemary, for garnish

*For the veal:*

2 (½-inch thick) veal T-bones, consisting of both strip
    and tenderloin
½ cup flour, seasoned with salt and pepper
2 beaten eggs
1 cup unseasoned bread crumbs
Canola oil
½ cup applesauce
2 whole red cherry peppers, sliced
Extra-virgin olive oil
Pinch of dried oregano
½ cup shredded cheese, like manchego,
    Grana Padano, or provolone

*For the sauce:*

2–3 tablespoons extra-virgin olive oil
½ red onion, sliced
1 clove garlic, chopped
8 shiitake mushrooms, sliced, stems removed
½ sliced apple
½ cup Marsala wine
1½ shots Averna (an Italian liqueur)
Salt and pepper
⅓ shot espresso
1 tablespoon chicken stock mixed with
    1 tablespoon flour to thicken

To make the veal: Dredge the veal in the flour mixture, then the beaten egg, and then the bread crumbs. Fill a skillet ¼ up the sides with canola oil and heat over medium heat until hot but not smoking. Add the veal and fry until golden, about 2–3 minutes on each side. Transfer to an oven-safe dish. Top with applesauce, cherry peppers, a drizzle of extra-virgin olive oil, the pinch of oregano, and the shredded cheese. Cook in a 500°F oven for about 10 minutes.

To make the sauce: Add olive oil to a saucepan and heat until hot, but not smoking. Add the red onion and garlic and cook until brown. Add mushrooms and apple and sauté until browned and cooked through. Add the Marsala and Averna, and salt and pepper to taste. When the sauce boils, add espresso. Add in the chicken stock mixture to thicken.

To finish: Throw the pork chop on a hot grill lightly greased with canola oil, and cook until medium/medium rare. Take the veal from the oven and place on a dish. Position the pork chop on top. Pour the sauce over, and garnish with a sprig of rosemary.

# Baccala-Style Lemon Sole a la Romana

(SERVES 2)

*For the fish:*

1½ pounds sole (or any flaky white fish) cut into
    6 equal-size logs
1 cup flour, seasoned with salt, pepper, and
    1 teaspoon chopped fresh parsley

*For the beer batter:*

½ cup heavy cream
1 cup flour
4 ounces beer
Canola oil, for frying

*For the sauce:*

3 tablespoons extra-virgin olive oil
½ clove garlic, sliced
1 shot white wine
Juice from ½ lemon, plus lemon slices for garnish
10–12 capers
½ teaspoon fresh parsley, chopped
Salt and pepper to taste
1 cup vegetable stock mixed with ½ cup flour

To make the fish: Combine heavy cream, flour, and beer. Dredge fish in seasoned flour, and then coat in the beer batter. Fill a 10-inch skillet ¼ of the way up the sides with canola oil. Heat until hot but not smoking. Add fish and fry until golden brown and crispy, about 1–2 minutes on each side. Set aside on paper towels to drain.

To make the sauce: Add olive oil to saucepan set over medium heat. Add in garlic, and sauté until golden. Add in the wine, lemon juice, capers, parsley, and salt and pepper. Bring to a boil. Slowly add in the stock and flour mixture, and cook to a medium thickness. Stack fish on a plate, and pour the sauce over. Garnish with sliced lemons.

# Sardinian-Style Shrimp with Spicy Marsala Sauce

(SERVES 2)

*For the shrimp:*

8 colossal shrimp, peeled, deveined, and butterflied
¼ cup flour, seasoned with salt and pepper
4 whole eggs, beaten
Canola oil, for frying

*For the sauce:*

2 tablespoons extra-virgin olive oil
1 clove garlic
1 Italian long hot pepper, diced
½ zucchini, cut into 6 planks
8 cremini mushrooms, cut into quarters
½ cup Marsala wine
¼ cup fig molasses, such as Artibel
   (can be found in specialty stores,
   like D. Coluccio and Sons)
Zest and juice from ¼ lemon
⅓ cup vegetable stock
1 tablespoon vegetable stock mixed with
   1 tablespoon flour, for thickening

To make the shrimp: Using a meat tenderizer or the palm of your hand, flatten the shrimp as you would scaloppine. Dredge them in the seasoned flour and dip them in the beaten egg. Fill a skillet with canola oil to about ¼ way up the sides. Heat over medium heat until hot but not smoking and add the shrimp. Fry until golden brown, about 2 minutes on each side. Remove to a paper towel to drain.

To make the sauce: In a large saucepan, add the olive oil and clove of garlic. Cook garlic until golden brown and remove from the oil. Add in the pepper, zucchini, and mushrooms, and sauté. When the vegetables are fully cooked, add the Marsala, fig molasses, lemon zest and juice, and the vegetable stock. When it comes to a good boil, add the shrimp to the sauce. Using a tablespoon, mix some of the stock and flour mixture into the sauce until just thickened.

# La Slowteria

548 Court Street, Carroll Gardens
(718) 858-2222
laslowteria.com
Chef/Owner: Hugo Orozco
Owner: Stephanie Heinegg de Orozco

One can hardly accuse Carroll Gardens of having too few noteworthy restaurants. Especially too few noteworthy seasonal restaurants. But noteworthy, seasonal Mexican restaurants? That's a new one for this corner of South Brooklyn.

Opened just over a year ago by Chef Hugo Orozco and his wife Stephanie Heinegg, La Slowteria combines the ethics of the Slow Food movement (local, sustainable, ethically sourced) with the flavors of Orozco's native Mexico. In fact, the restaurant serves as a replica of the spot Orozco owned in the resort town of Tulum, except instead of six adjoining cabanas on the beach, La Slowteria occupies an intimate space on Court Street. And Orozco has to look a little farther for the ingredients he uses; gone are the days when fishermen delivered him their daily catch, straight from the docks. "Of course, it's difficult to be entirely local right away. For example, I would love to have a community contact for avocados," Orozco says. "But this takes time. I don't recommend getting married, changing your country, and opening a restaurant within six months!"

You'd never know he was under any sort of duress. The dining room is as relaxed as a yoga retreat, and dishes like La Mano, lime juice-cured scallops arranged on paper-thin slices of cucumber, are unfailingly fresh and pristine. La Slowteria is a restaurant borne of the idyllic Mayan Riviera, yes, but ultimately, it's also perfectly suited for the eco-minded enclave of Carroll Gardens. "We're really looking to make contacts in the neighborhood. Right after we opened, Rob Newton from Seersucker came over, and took me to the local greenmarket. I respect that," Orozco says. "I love the idea of working together, supporting each other, and creating a beautiful restaurant family here in Brooklyn."

# La Mano

(SERVES 4)

10 fresh scallops

4 limes

½ teaspoon fresh ground black pepper

1 teaspoon coarse sea salt

1 medium red onion, julienned

¼ cup chopped cilantro

2 cucumbers

2 ripe avocados

12 corn tostadas

*For the raw green salsa:*

1 lime

2 garlic cloves

¼ cup chopped cilantro

2 green tomatoes

¼ red onion

½ tablespoon coarse sea salt

½ teaspoon black pepper

1 serrano pepper (without seeds)

Cucumber cores

*For the piquin chile oil:*

2 tablespoons olive oil

2 tablespoons dried chile piquin

2 garlic cloves

½ teaspoon salt

1 lime

Cut the scallops horizontally in order to have 20 pieces and use 5 halves per serving. Place them in a bowl, juice 4 limes over the scallops, and sprinkle with fresh ground pepper. Add the salt, red onion, and cilantro and mix well with a spoon. Let the mixture rest for about 5 minutes. Using a mandoline or peeler, slice the cucumber lengthwise, rotating it to avoid the core and its seeds (reserve these cores). Place the thin slices to the side. Cut the avocados in half and remove the pit. Using a large round spoon, scoop out each avocado, keeping its shape intact, and remove it from its shell. With a knife, cut the bottom of each half to make it flat so the avocado does not wobble when placed on a plate.

To make the salsa: In a food processor, place all of the raw ingredients, including the cores of the cucumber from before, and blend until the sauce is smooth. Add 8 tablespoons of the sauce to the bowl of scallops, mixing it with a spoon, and let it sit another 2–3 minutes.

To make the chile oil: Heat the oil and fry the chiles lightly until they are crispy. Place chiles in a mortar, add the garlic, salt, and lime and grind until it becomes a paste. Set the paste aside to cool.

To serve: On a cold plate, lay 5 slices of cucumber in the shape of a hand with a scallop half at the top of each slice. Place the avocado half at the base ("palm" of the hand) and stuff the opening with the remaining mixture of salsa and julienned onions. Using the bottom of a small spoon smear a line of the piquin oil next to the hand on the side of the plate so your guests can decide on how spicy they want their dish to be. Serve with a corn tostada on the side.

# Leske's Bakery

7612 5th Avenue, Bay Ridge
(718) 680-2323
LESKESBAKERY.COM
Head Baker: Stephen Howe

Bay Ridge is no longer the Scandinavian stronghold it once was. But the changing face of the neighborhood has done little to dampen the affection for Leske's, which has been making traditional favorites like *boller, kringler,* and (practically a prerequisite for any NYC-based bakery) a mean black and white cookie for over fifty years.

"It's been like an icon in the neighborhood," says longtime head baker Stephen Howe. "Especially now that there's nothing around here like it. Even people who have moved out of Bay Ridge still come back for our *kransekake* and doughnuts and danish. We're pretty unique, and a little bit old fashioned. And people love that."

From kitchen staff to counter crew to the easily identifiable blue and yellow Leske's logo, the shop remains essentially unchanged, save the recent addition of a few new high-end ovens. The bakery also does its best to hew as closely as possible to recession-era prices (and keep nostalgic taste buds satiated) by faithfully sticking to time-honored recipes. That means no highfalutin organics, fancy fudge frostings, or whole-fruit fillings if the original didn't distinctly require it.

"Business is business, but we're all a family here. We want this shop to be successful for everyone, and that includes our customers," says Howe.

The Bay Ridge faithful may be more open to wine bars, gourmet groceries, and farm-to-table fare than they once were—but when it comes to *fyrstekakes* and limpa bread, they also know better than to mess with a winning recipe.

# BOLLER

(MAKES 4 DOZEN)

Baker's Note: Boller should be moderately yeasty, with a lightly sweet taste. Freshly ground cardamom yields best results. King Arthur makes both clear and high gluten flours; when combined, they create an ideal elasticity in the dough.

1 quart water
3 eggs
1 tablespoon salt
1½ cups granulated sugar
1½ cups shortening
¾ cup fresh yeast
¾ cup powdered milk
8 cups clear flour
8 cups high-gluten flour
½ cup ground cardamom
8 cups raisins

Add water and eggs together in the large bowl of an electric mixer. Then add all the dry ingredients except for the raisins. Mix on medium to medium-high speed (#3) with mixing hook until all the dough pulls away from the bowl. Add raisins and mix again until raisins are well distributed.

Cover bowl with clean towel and place in warm area until it doubles in size, about 1½ hours. Knock down the dough and allow to rise again to double size, approximately 1½ hours more. Dough is now ready to use. The dough can be cut into a variety of sizes, typically about 2 ounces, but any size can work.

Cut and round dough by hand and place on baking sheet. For a darker exterior, coat dough balls with an egg wash before baking.

Bake at 400°F for 15–18 minutes until brown. Allow to rest while cooling.

# Littleneck

288 3rd Avenue, Gowanus
(718) 522-1921
LITTLENECKBROOKLYN.COM
Owners: Aaron Lefkove and Andy Curtin

Theoretically, Littleneck should never have worked out. Who opens a New England–style clam shack a stone's throw from the murky Gowanus Canal, in a largely industrial neighborhood with a bare minimum of foot traffic? That would be Aaron Lefkove and Andy Curtin, two friends and former bandmates with no prior restaurant experience to speak of . . . practically a liability in and of itself. "It started as a casual conversation at a backyard barbecue. Andy and I were grilling steamer clams, and we starting talking about how you couldn't really find them anywhere in Brooklyn," explains Lefkove. "It snowballed from a kernel of an idea, "we should do something like this," into "oh my god, we're actually doing this!"

The pair wound up taking an almost entirely DIY approach when it came to refurbishing their space, raising over $13,000 from the crowd-funding website Kickstarter. And they spent most of it on reclaimed, recycled, and eco-friendly furniture and materials—practically the blueprint for fledgling restaurants nowadays. "It was kind of a perfect storm of circumstances that allowed us to realize our dream without breaking the bank," Lefkove admitted. "At the time we signed our lease, we were one of the first restaurants to open in Gowanus. But the neighborhood was also on the verge of changing; there was a contingent of artists here, and plain industrial space being converted over to more creative uses. So we're grateful to have been able to get in on the ground floor, and we didn't need a million dollars to do it."

# Lobster Roll

(SERVES 4)

Owner's Note: The lobster roll at Littleneck is made from fresh, live lobsters, which we bring in, poach, and break down daily in our kitchen. We never use frozen or processed meat. Our rolls are made in a simple, traditional New England style, piled high with lobster coated in a very light mayo-based dressing.

4 live lobsters (approx. 1½ pounds each)
Kosher salt
4 tablespoons mayonnaise
1 lemon, halved
1 stalk of celery, diced
Split-top hot dog buns
Butter
Lemon slices, for garnish
Pickles, for garnish

Fill a large stock pot with water and a liberal dash of kosher salt. Fill a kitchen sink or large basin with ice and water. Boil all 4 lobsters for about 7½ minutes or until they turn bright red, being very careful not to overcook (I cannot stress this part enough!).

When the lobsters are fully cooked, remove them from the pot and shock them in the ice water to stop the cooking. Once the lobsters are fully cooled, separate the tails, knuckles, and claws. You can discard the lobster bodies or save them to make stock, however, you will not need them for the rest of this recipe.

Once you have separated all the pieces, use a pair of kitchen shears to break down individual knuckles and claws and remove the meat. When breaking down the tails, you want to remove and discard the green and black roe. Once you have separated out all the meat and discarded the shells, give the knuckles and tails a coarse chop. Save the claws for later.

In a mixing bowl, add mayonnaise, a pinch of kosher salt, the juice from half a lemon, the diced celery (this is a matter of personal preference with regard to how much celery to add—at Littleneck they add roughly 1 teaspoon per roll), and the lobster meat, including the unchopped claws. Lightly stir with a spoon until the meat is coated completely.

Butter the hot dog buns on both sides, and lightly toast them on a griddle or stovetop. Fill the buns with the knuckle and tail meat and add a claw or two on top. Garnish with a slice of lemon and pickles and serve!

Jewish food is a lot of things. Comforting. Steeped in tradition. A no-fail fattening agent for concerned grandmas the world over. What it is not, one would think, is stylish. Until now. Some of Brooklyn's coolest—and youngest—members of the tribe are spinning Bubby's old recipes into gastronomic gold, taking schmaltz-laden warhorses like latkes, matzoh balls, chopped liver, and even gefilte fish to new culinary heights.

**Mile End** (97A Hoyt Street; 718-852-7510; mileenddeli.com): It's odd to think that young guns like Rae Cohen and Noah Bernamoff could ever be considered the forefathers of anything, but corned beef and kasha varnishkes weren't exactly chic before they opened their Boerum Hill delicatessen in 2010. Like it or not, these Montrealites have shaped the cuisine of the New Brooklyn Jew, with house-smoked, sustainably

sourced meat, homemade pickles, and unexpected specials like oxtail kreplach with mushroom broth and chile oil.

**Traif** (9229 South 4th Street; 347-844-9578; traifny.com): Although Chef/Owner Jason Marcus takes plenty of pride in his Jewish roots, he joyfully flouts kosher living at his cozy Williamsburg eatery, Traif. Some dishes would make the grade for Passover—a salad of roasted carrots, apples, raisins, feta, greens, and sunflower seeds—others decidedly would not, such as his signature foie gras with ham chips, and chopped chicken livers with bacon/balsamic toasts. See p. 190.

**Shelsky's Smoked Fish** (251 Smith Street; 718-855-8817; shelskys.com): This Cobble Hill shop assures that Brooklynites will no longer have to travel to the Lower East Side in search of Jewish appetizing stores of yore. And although owner Peter Shelsky pays homage to the classics—like belly lox, whitefish salad, borscht, and kippered herring—he puts his chef's training to work with Manischewitz-braised short ribs, clementine/ginger rugelach, and celeriac and sweet potato kugel. See p. 170.

**The Gefilteria** (gefilteria.com): Even while riding high on a new wave of Eastern European love, "gourmetizing" gefilte fish—one of the most oft reviled foods in the Jewish culinary canon—seems like a tall order. But this Brooklyn-based online store uses Great Lakes–caught salmon, pike, and whitefish, making layered loaves that are a far cry from the gray, unidentifiable lozenges submerged in the suspicious, quivery gel most of us remember.

**Danny Macaroons** (dannymacaroons.com): Jewish pastries may be a much easier sell than pickled cabbage and gefilte fish, but that doesn't mean they're all created equal. Danny Macaroons—available online, or at Smorgasburg, in season—are neither gummy nor dry, and come in categorically nontraditional flavors such as red velvet, roasted almond, German chocolate, and sea-salt caramel.

# MILL BASIN KOSHER DELICATESSEN

5823 AVE T, MILL BASIN
(718) 241-4910
MILLBASINDELI.COM
OWNERS: MARK AND JORDAN SCHACHNER

Opened in 1974, Mill Basin Delicatessen is one of the oldest surviving kosher delis in Brooklyn. And Jordan Schachner (son of owner, Mark) was essentially born into the business. "I used to break up the hot dogs, back when they came attached in links. I cleared tables, became a waiter, worked downstairs in the kitchen, and pretty much had every job until I got to the top. Now I'm officially married to the deli," he smiles ruefully.

It's certainly put Schachner in a position to watch the neighborhood change over the years, from Eastern European enclave—packed with places peddling corned beef, pastrami, matzoh balls, knishes and kasha varnishkas ("There must have been forty or fifty delis within twenty miles of here," Schachner theorizes)—to a melting pot of ethnicities, including, ironically, a recent influx of religious Jews. "They usually don't eat here because we're open on Friday and Saturday. We're not glatt kosher, which is the higher level of kosher," Schachner explains. "So yeah, there are only two or three delis left in Brooklyn. And we're the big one."

But something that hasn't changed (besides the recipe for a killer stuffed cabbage, that is) is Mill Basin's museum-quality collection of modern art—which adds an unexpectedly contemporary element to the decidedly old-school eatery.

"My dad started collecting about eight years into the deli. We had a bunch of Ertés here, which got stolen," Schachner recalls. "The dealer tried to sell him some more for not such a good price, and my dad is not shy; he's got a big mouth from Brooklyn. And the guy was actually from Brooklyn, so he respected my father for opening his big mouth and he ended up doing the right thing, and they formed a relationship from there."

In addition to the 125 Ertés, the restaurant gallery includes works by Chagall, Mucha, Lichtenstein, and James Rizzi, all of which Schachner oversees, now that his father has taken a step back from the business. "My grandparents had a kosher deli on Avenue C, and my father worked there as a child. He had the same issues that I did—couldn't work side by side with his parents," laughs Schachner. "Me and my father bang heads a lot. So if he were working in the deli now, I probably wouldn't be here. I have the same attitude I learned from him; I'm just like him. Of course, he ended up leaving his father's deli and going out on his own!"

# STUFFED CABBAGE

(SERVES 6–8)

1 large young head cabbage
1 cup tomato puree
2 cups water
1½ cup sugar
1 teaspoon kosher salt
½ teaspoon garlic powder
1 teaspoon white pepper, divided
2 cups sauerkraut
3 lemons, chopped into ½-inch pieces, pits removed
2 pounds ground beef
1 large onion, finely chopped
2 cups cooked rice
¼ cup matzoh meal
1 teaspoon salt

Cut the cabbage in half and core it. Pull off the large leaves, and cut out the thick center stem. Pat the leaves dry with towels. Coarsely chop the remaining small leaves and use them to line the pan, so the bottoms of the cabbage rolls don't burn. Reserve a few of the larger leaves for later.

Add the tomato puree and water to a large saucepan; set over medium heat. Bring to a boil, and add sugar, kosher salt, garlic powder, white pepper, sauerkraut, and lemons. Reduce heat

and simmer for 60–90 minutes, until the sauce reaches your desired thickness. Add more sugar or lemon juice for the sweet-sour taste you prefer. Set sauce aside. Take out lemon pieces.

In a large bowl, mix ground beef, chopped onion, rice, matzo meal, 1 teaspoon salt and ½ teaspoon white pepper, mixing thoroughly. Don't overmix, or the meat will become tough.

Place about ½ cup of meat on each large cabbage leaf. Roll away from you to encase the meat. Flip the right side of the leaf to the middle, then flip the left side. You will have something that looks like an envelope. Once again, roll away from you to create a neat little package. Arrange cabbage rolls, seam-side down, on top of the chopped cabbage leaves in as many layers as necessary. Add 1 quart water. Cover stuffed cabbage with the reserved large cabbage leaves, and a layer of aluminum foil. Bake at 375°F for 1½ hours.

Remove from the oven and let cool. Put sauce in a pot, add cabbage rolls, and heat on top of the stove. If sauce has thinned a bit, you can heat up sauce with the rolls on a low flame until the sauce thickens to your liking.

# MIMI'S HUMMUS

1209 CORTELYOU ROAD, FLATBUSH
(718) 284-4444
MIMISHUMMUS.COM
OWNER: MIMI KITANI

With scruffy brick apartment complexes giving way to sprawling Victorian mansions, and a tiny concentration of well-regarded restaurants dotting Cortelyou Road, low-key Ditmas Park is consistently described as one of Brooklyn's up-and-coming neighborhoods. And considering she owns two of the six most talked-about local food businesses (Mimi's Hummus and the simply named Market, an adjoining gourmet goods shop), Mimi Kitani has played a large part in furthering its appeal. "No one believes me, but it all just happened!" Kitani protests, when asked about her role as restaurateur. "I was working at The Farm on Adderley (the area's first destination restaurant), and I saw this space. I knew the neighborhood. It just seemed right."

Not that she went from server to shop owner with no real game plan. Born in Israel, Kitani wanted to give a new face to Middle Eastern food, showcasing a side of the cuisine well beyond the expected falafel and shawarma. "I felt like there was so much Middle Eastern food around, but not the kind I love to eat," explains Kitani, sprawling in the sun on a bench between her storefronts. "I wanted to cook food like my grandmother made . . . simple, clean, and healthy, but still delicious, warm, and comforting. I wanted to give something of me to other people."

And although Kitani expectedly draws raves for her hummus (little more than an emulsion of freshly cooked chickpeas and nutty tahini), the virtuous cauliflower salad is an equally appropriate mission statement for her restaurant. "It's super healthy. Some people call it vegan, which I honestly never considered whether it was or not," she says. "But the secret to this salad, like with any recipe, is just to make it your own. Don't be afraid to use your hands and taste it, alter it. That's the true pleasure of cooking."

## CAULIFLOWER SALAD

(SERVES 4)

1 medium-size fresh cauliflower

Olive oil

½ cup tahini dressing (see ingredients below)

5 tablespoons lemon juice

1 chopped garlic clove

½ cup chopped parsley

1 teaspoon kosher salt

*For tahini dressing:*

2 crushed garlic cloves

2 tablespoons lemon juice

1 cup tahini

Pinch of salt

½ cup of ice cold water

Preheat the oven to 350°F. Cut the cauliflower head into small florets. Mix the cauliflower with some salt and olive oil and roast in the oven for about 30–35 minutes. While the cauliflower is roasting put together all of the tahini ingredients; garlic, lemon juice, tahini, and salt. Gradually add the water until it becomes smooth and silky.

In a mixing bowl, combine ½ cup of the tahini dressing (you can refrigerate the tahini that's left and use it as a spread) with the lemon juice, chopped garlic, parsley, and salt and mix together. Add the cold roasted cauliflower and mix with your hand until evenly mixed.

# Northeast Kingdom

18 Wyckoff Avenue, Bushwick
(718) 386-3864
north-eastkingdom.com
Owner: Paris Smeraldo
Chef: Kevin Adey

Paris Smeraldo not only supplies his rustic Bushwick restaurant with eggs and veggies brought down from his farm in the Hudson Valley, but also the roots, leaves, and berries he forages each week with his very own hands. "Many restaurants say they're doing foraging these days, but it really just means that they're buying things from foragers," says Smeraldo. "I grew up in the woods of Vermont with no running water or electricity, so I was indoctrinated with learning about wild foods from a very young age."

That means the industrious owner can frequently be found gathering elderberry blooms for cordials and cocktails, scouring streambeds for ramps, climbing black locust trees to nab their edible flowers, and weeding his garden bed for wood sorrel, lamb's-

quarters, dandelion leaves, and garlic mustard. "The stuff that I have the privilege of using here, I've never seen in a restaurant in sixteen years," Chef Kevin Adey asserts. "Foraging in springtime is easy, but who wants to tramp around the woods in the cold looking for black trumpet mushrooms? That really separates the men from the boys."

Northeast Kingdom's back-to-the-land approach also extends to using whole animals, which is why you'll find expected dishes, like pork tenderloin, followed by more unusual menu items, like pigs head terrine. "The most important thing we do is utilize everything, and that ends with the pig head," says Adey. "It's actually an extremely flavorful piece of meat, because the muscles in the head do so much work. And honestly, if I didn't tell you it was pig's head, you'd think it was pork shoulder."

# This Morning's Farm Egg, Pig's Head Terrine, Fish-Sauce Caramel & Thai Chile

(CARAMEL AND TERRINE YIELD 30 PORTIONS. POACH EGGS TO ORDER AS NEEDED)

*For caramel:*

2 cups sugar
1 bottle (25 ounces) fish sauce
1 medium white onion, sliced
1 tablespoon ground black pepper

*For pig's head terrine:*

1 pig head
Salt and pepper
2 quarts rough-cut mirepoix (carrots, celery, onion)
Water
1 cup reserved braising liquid

*For serving:*

1 pound brussels sprouts
Canola oil
3 scallions, sliced
Fresh lime juice
Salt and pepper
Eggs, poached
Sliced Thai chiles

To make the caramel: Over high heat, melt sugar in a deep saucepan. Right before it burns (some color is ok), deglaze the pan by whisking in the fish sauce, being careful not to splatter. Add onion and black pepper. Reduce heat to simmer for 5 minutes, or until the onions are soft. Set aside to cool.

To make the terrine: Season the pig head liberally with salt and pepper. Place in a large pan with mirepoix, and cover with water. Cover and bake overnight (12 hours) at 250°F. When cool enough to handle, shred the meat and fat. Season to taste with salt and pepper. Add 1 cup braising liquid and mix well. Place mixture in plastic wrap and roll into a log. Chill overnight.

To serve: Remove the outer leaves from the brussels sprouts and cut them into quarters. Add the sprouts to a sauté pan, coat with canola oil, and cook until tender and crispy. Combine brussels sprouts and scallions. Season with lime juice, salt, and pepper. Place on a dish or in a bowl. Poach egg and slice the pig's head terrine. Place terrine slice and poached egg on top of brussels sprouts. Drizzle with the fish-sauce caramel and garnish with sliced Thai chiles, or dried crushed red pepper.

Did you know some of the city's best eats are growing in the cracks of the streets? Foraging for food might sound like something humanity outgrew around the same time we domesticated livestock, but Northeast Kingdom's Paris Smeraldo says it's actually a fun and easy way to find delicious food. "There's probably wood sorrel and garlic mustard growing within three blocks of wherever you are right now," he said. "It's as simple as going out with a bowl, being comfortable identifying what's edible, and making a salad for yourself."

Here are some local foods to be on the lookout for—but be careful and consult an expert before you eat anything you find on the ground!

**Wood Sorrel:** Looks a lot like clover but has very distinct heart-shaped leaves. The teeny yellow flowers have a lemony, acidic flavor that goes really well in salad.

**Garlic Mustard:** Garlic mustard produces small clusters of flowers that are easy to collect and are plentiful. Use them as a simple garnish on red meat dishes or toss into a quick sauté with greens.

**Black Locust:** The flowers that appear on black locust trees are around for only a few weeks. They grow in clusters and eaten directly off the tree have a sweet, sugar snap pea flavor—toss around liberally in salads or as garnish.

**Elderflower:** Look for a small tree or large shrub usually 8–14 feet high, growing in open full sunlight. Look for large, snowy-white, flat-top flower clusters, which are fragrant. It's not uncommon to find them in parks and on the roadside.

**Stinging Nettles:** Nettles are some of the first greens to come up in the spring, and are packed with healthful properties like easily digestible amino acids, iron, and vitamin C. They work well in soup or as a tea.

**Dandelion Greens:** Dandelion greens grow all summer long, but are best in early spring when they're the most tender and least bitter. Sauté, or use young greens raw in a salad.

**Lamb's-Quarters:** This tender, mild green is wonderful raw as a salad component or as a garnish. Lamb's-quarters grow in areas with disturbed soil, and flourish in a poorly tended garden. The under-leaves have a striking magenta hue. They can grow to over 4 feet high, and the tender tops can be harvested throughout the summer.

# OVENLY

31 GREENPOINT AVENUE, GREENPOINT
(347) 689-3608
OVEN.LY
OWNERS: ERIN PATINKIN AND AGATHA KULAGA

We see book clubs as an opportunity to drink wine and unembarrassedly analyze *Fifty Shades of Grey*. But in the case of Erin Patinkin and Agatha Kulaga, they can also serve as launching pads for highly successful food businesses. "We actually met at a very food-focused book club, frequented by a lot of professional women in the industry," Patinkin remembers. "And when I met Agatha, I told her how surprised I was that a business hadn't come out of the group. Everyone was so talented, and so interested in the same things."

"She told me she had been trying to start something for some time, and we just began batting around ideas," Patinkin continues, "and Ovenly kind of naturally evolved as one of them."

The pair started out by making gourmet bar snacks (spicy bacon caramel corn and Old Bay and Worcestershire-spiced peanuts are consistent best-sellers), which they supplied to places like Brooklyn Brewery and Veronica People's Club. But it was their sweet and savory pastries, fragrant with herbs, frequently nut-based, and inspired by

their Eastern European backgrounds, that eventually became the heart of a full-fledged bakery in Greenpoint.

"Agatha's parents are from Poland and my grandparents were from Poland and Austria, so we had exposure to desserts that are a little less saccharine," Patinkin says. "We just really like interesting combinations of sweet, salty, and spice." Think apricot scones, black caraway shortbread, pistachio cardamom cupcakes and hazelnut cookies, a naturally gluten-free treat accented by orange zest, maple sugar, and whole hazelnuts.

"The other thing about our baking is that everything is natural. Even if our flavor combinations are unique, there's nothing in there that's overwhelming," Patinkin assures. "And that's so true of those cookies. They're very simple to make, and yet, not something you see every day."

# HAZELNUT MAPLE COOKIES
(MAKES 24 COOKIES)

4⅓ cups hazelnuts
1 cup granulated white sugar
Zest of 1 small orange or tangerine
1 tablespoon maple syrup
3 egg whites
Maple sugar for rolling (found in specialty stores, greenmarkets, or online)
Whole hazelnuts, cut into halves for decoration

Preheat oven to 350°F. Pulse hazelnuts in a food processor until they form a coarse meal. Pieces should not be larger than about ⅛-inch in diameter. Transfer hazelnut meal to a bowl. Add sugar, zest, maple syrup, and egg whites. Using a rubber spatula or gloved hands, mix ingredients together until they are very well combined. Cover the dough with plastic wrap and let rest for 10 minutes at room temperature, or until the dough is slightly dry to the touch. Using your hands or a small cookie scoop (recommended), form dough into balls that are 1½-inches in diameter. Roll cookies in maple sugar and top with half a hazelnut by pressing the nut into dough. Bake for 12 minutes. Let cool completely.

# Parish Hall

109A North 3rd Street, Williamsburg
(718) 782-2602
PARISHHALL.NET
Chef: Evan Hanczor

The American South is known for fried chicken, collard greens, and shrimp and grits. The West Coast claims fish tacos, cioppino, cobb salad, and sourdough bread. The Great Lakes region chows down on fried cheese curds, deep-dish pizza, and Cincinnati chili. So what's the defining cuisine here in the Northeast?

"It's been an ongoing process trying to figure that out," says Evan Hanczor, chef at hyper-regional restaurant Parish Hall. "The Northeast has served as such an entry point for people migrating to this country that the cuisine here continues to evolve and change. So we're really trying to focus on ingredients that are constants in this region, or that grow here naturally, and witness how they express themselves on the plate."

At Parish Hall, that means steering clear of existing culinary traditions—for instance, you won't find Hudson Valley duck transformed into Italian Bolognese—and presenting straight-up amalgams of local dairy, grains, proteins, and produce, like chilled nettle soup with trout roe and radish and roasted chicken over Cayuga barley and wild mustard.

And it certainly doesn't hurt that owner George Weld has a farm in upstate New York to furnish such an edible exploration—sending truly homegrown fruits and vegetables straight to the dinner plates of Parish Hall's patrons. "Goatfell Farm is part of the inspiration for what the restaurant came to be. Having hands-on experience growing vegetables, raising animals for eggs, and meeting farmers absolutely affects the way we think about food here, and allows us to try new things," says Hanczor. "If we read about a certain variety of bean or tomato that grows well in the Northeast region, we can use the farm."

"Two years ago, we got in touch with people who were developing a variety of potatoes specifically for New York soil, and we were able to take some of those potatoes and test them," he adds. "I hope every time we make a new dish, we really come closer to having something to say about this area."

# VEGETABLES & DUMPLINGS

### (SERVES 4–6)

Chef's Note: One of the main things we've tried to focus on here from the beginning is using more vegetables. And for that reason, this dish is very emblematic of the restaurant. It also translates really easily to the home kitchen because you can make the cheese broth a few days before, and the dumplings are really versatile.

**4 cups seasonal vegetables**

*For the dumplings:*

½ tablespoon salt
1 teaspoon sugar
12 ounces (3 sticks) butter
3 cups water
3¾ cups unbleached flour
11 whole eggs

*For the cheese broth:*

1 cup sliced shallots
2 cloves garlic, sliced
1 tablespoon butter
½ teaspoon chile flakes
1½ tablespoons lovage stem or chopped celery
1 dried apple core or 1 whole apple, chopped
1 quart water
1 quart vegetable stock
2 cups cheese rinds
1 sprig thyme
Salt and pepper

*For serving:*

4 tablespoons butter
1 shallot, minced
Salt and pepper

To prepare the vegetables: Use 4 cups of whichever seasonal vegetables you enjoy. In the winter, roast cubed root vegetables ahead of time and add some kale. In the spring, use ramps, radishes, asparagus, and spinach. In the summer, add tomatoes, peppers, and chard. Always use a nice mix of vegetables, cut roughly bite-size, and try to include at least one leafy green, such as kale or chard.

To make the dumplings: Combine salt, sugar, and butter in a stock pot with water. Bring to a boil and simmer until butter is melted. When butter is melted, add all flour at once and stir vigorously over medium heat until dough begins to pull away from sides of pot and form a clean ball. Continue to stir over low heat for another minute or two. Place dough in mixing bowl and beat with the paddle mixer on medium speed. Add eggs one at a time, beating until all eggs have been added and are well incorporated. Let dough cool. When cooled, form small ovals with tablespoons and poach in simmering cheese broth for 1–2 minutes. Remove from broth for serving later.

To make the broth: Sweat shallot and garlic in butter over medium heat until softened and lightly colored. Add remaining ingredients. Simmer gently 30–40 minutes until broth is rich and cheesy. Season lightly with salt and pepper.

To serve: Add butter to a large pan, placed over medium heat. Add dumplings (without crowding) and brown on all sides, cooking in batches if necessary. Add the minced shallot and cook until translucent. Divide dumplings and shallots between four to six soup bowls. Top each serving with ¼ cup vegetables and ¼ cup cheese broth. Season with salt and pepper as needed and serve hot!

# PAULIE GEE'S

60 GREENPOINT AVENUE, GREENPOINT
(347) 987-3747
PAULIEGEE.COM
OWNER: PAULIE GEE

"Have I seen you before? I know you," says Paulie Gee, stopping at the table of a redheaded young woman during dinner service. "First time? You must be an actress. No? She looks like an actress—it's a compliment," he assures, turning to her date.

As Paulie continues to work the floor, greeting old friends and welcoming others, it reminds everyone—from the cluster already gathered by the hostess table to those grouped in the waiting room, crowding the entrance, or overflowing through the big barnyard doors and out onto the street, why the heck they're willing to wait so long for pizza on a Friday night.

And yes, a lot of the credit goes to those gorgeous, thin-crusted pies that emerge like clockwork every few seconds from the depths of a custom-designed, wood-burning oven. But the lion's share of acclaim belongs squarely with Paulie himself, a southern Brooklyn native (from the neighborhood now called Kensington), and former IT consultant who found his real calling late in life. "When I was at work, I would be daydreaming about entertaining people on the weekends," he remembers. "Everyone was saying I should open a restaurant, but this is New York. The greatest chefs in the world are here; I can't compete with them. But with pizza, you have an oven, you chop stuff up, you put it on top, and that's it!"

"So I decided I was going to build an oven at home and practice, because I had to prove to myself I could do it," Paulie continues. "I wanted to make sure that if I had a restaurant, and a girlfriend I knew from high school came in, I'd be really proud to show it off." He certainly deserves props for his astounding metamorphosis from office worker to backyard pizza hobbyist to full-blown, well-respected pizzaiolo and restaurateur. It's obvious now, surrounded by hip Greenpoint couples and young families, Brooklyn natives, and Jersey out-of-towners, that this is where Paulie Gee was meant to be—lavishing equal attention on his customers, and on the food he serves them.

So how in the world do you even begin to replicate the "Feel Like Bacon Love" pie at home, worthy of the Paulie Gee stamp of approval? "Be very careful when you're stirring; don't let the onion break up with bacon. And don't you dare, whoever you are, even think about using anything other than salted butter!" he admonishes. I don't want to hear about no margarine."

# "FEEL LIKE BACON LOVE" PIZZA

(MAKES 1 PIE)

4 ounces fresh mozzarella
1 (16-ounce) can Italian peeled tomatoes
½ large Vidalia onion
⅓ pound thick-sliced smoked bacon
4 ounces (1 stick) salted butter
1 round of pizza dough, approximately ½ pound
Freshly ground black pepper

Shred the mozzarella and place in a small covered bowl. Remove tomatoes from the puree in the can, place in a blender, and puree.

Place the pureed tomatoes in a medium saucepan and heat over a medium flame. Once it comes to a slow boil, lower the flame and add the onion, bacon, and butter. Stir gently so as not to break apart the onion. Continue to simmer until the sauce thickens, about 35 minutes.

Carefully remove the onion and bacon strips.

Stretch the dough to about 12 inches. Place two large spoons of sauce on the stretched dough. Place the shredded mozzarella on the pie. Bake the pizza in the oven until cheese starts to brown slightly. Grind black pepper on top.

Slice and serve.

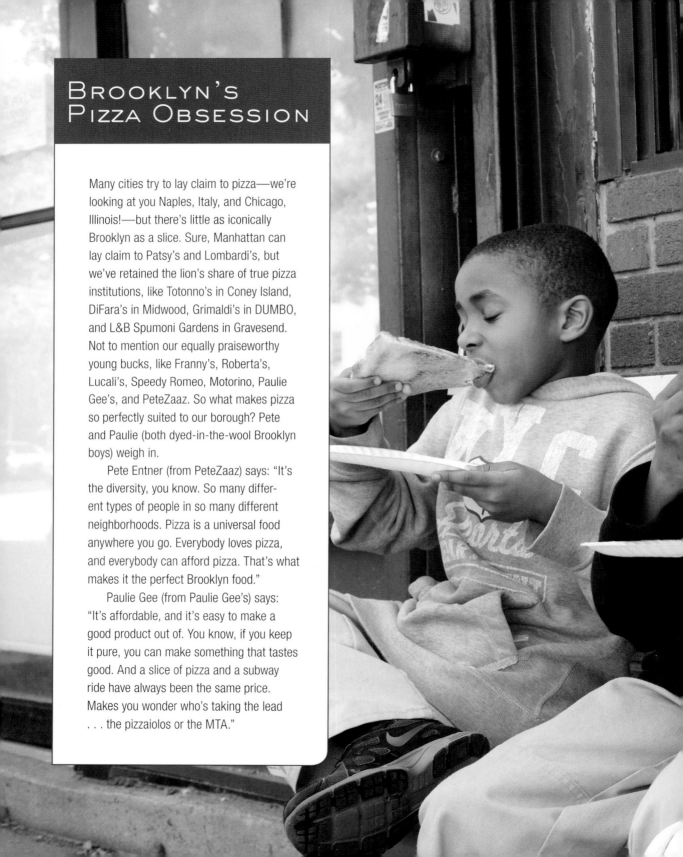

# BROOKLYN'S PIZZA OBSESSION

Many cities try to lay claim to pizza—we're looking at you Naples, Italy, and Chicago, Illinois!—but there's little as iconically Brooklyn as a slice. Sure, Manhattan can lay claim to Patsy's and Lombardi's, but we've retained the lion's share of true pizza institutions, like Totonno's in Coney Island, DiFara's in Midwood, Grimaldi's in DUMBO, and L&B Spumoni Gardens in Gravesend. Not to mention our equally praiseworthy young bucks, like Franny's, Roberta's, Lucali's, Speedy Romeo, Motorino, Paulie Gee's, and PeteZaaz. So what makes pizza so perfectly suited to our borough? Pete and Paulie (both dyed-in-the-wool Brooklyn boys) weigh in.

Pete Entner (from PeteZaaz) says: "It's the diversity, you know. So many different types of people in so many different neighborhoods. Pizza is a universal food anywhere you go. Everybody loves pizza, and everybody can afford pizza. That's what makes it the perfect Brooklyn food."

Paulie Gee (from Paulie Gee's) says: "It's affordable, and it's easy to make a good product out of. You know, if you keep it pure, you can make something that tastes good. And a slice of pizza and a subway ride have always been the same price. Makes you wonder who's taking the lead . . . the pizzaiolos or the MTA."

# PEOPLE'S POPS

808 UNION STREET, PARK SLOPE
(347) 850-2388
PEOPLESPOPS.COM
OWNERS: DAVID CARRELL, JOEL HOROWITZ, AND NATHALI JORDI

It's amazing who you can find on Craigslist.

In David Carrell's case, the free classifieds website connected him with Joel Horowitz, his eventual business partner at People's Pops, one of the greatest success stories to come out of the Brooklyn Flea and Smorgasburg to date. "We were Craigslist roommates. We screamed at each other, we realized we weren't good to live together, but it turns out we were good to start a business together," laughs Carrell. The third member of the artisanal popsicle dream team is Carrell's childhood friend and former prom date, Nathali Jordi—whose passion for the local and sustainable food movement set them on the path to creating the perfect pop.

"It just started as a one-day experiment. Why should this simple, guilt-free treat taste like cough medicine?" Carrell remembers. "We poured fresh fruit puree into Dixie Cups, brought them to the New Amsterdam Market, and they sold out in two hours. We showed up at the Brooklyn Flea in its second week, and we've been there ever since. And now, six years later, we're in multiple markets and have our first Brooklyn storefront."

That would be on Union Street in Park Slope, surrounded by young kids and families, the perfect focus group for their seasonally rotating menu of ice pops and shave-ice (all made with locally grown fruit and herbs, of course). It's a simple equation that's brought them tremendous success . . . but what if you'd still prefer to make your own popsicles at home?

"Remember when you were a kid pouring orange juice in the ice tray, and you checked it every hour and when you pulled it out it tasted shardy and bad?" posits Carrell. "The speed of the freeze is important. Put your pops in the back bottom of your freezer and don't open it."

"The other important factor is to use puree, forget about juice," he continues, brandishing a rose-colored honey- and chamomile-flavored pop, shot through with chunks of fresh peach. "Just blend up some fruit, and put pieces of pear or strawberry in there. You don't want that watered-down, icy taste that makes your teeth squeak when you bite down." He takes a nibble of the popsicle and shivers. "It grosses me out just thinking about it."

## PEACH, HONEY & CHAMOMILE ICE POP

(MAKES 10 POPS)

4 tree-ripened yellow peaches
2 slightly soft white peaches
¼ cup fresh honey, plus extra for adjusting sweetness
2 tablespoons freshly squeezed lemon juice
Pinch of kosher salt
1 bouquet fresh chamomile flowers

Rinse, halve, and pit two-thirds of the peaches, and puree them (skin and all) until the mixture is almost smooth. Transfer to a container with a pouring spout and stir the honey, lemon juice, salt, and three finely minced chamomile flowers in with the pureed peaches. Coarsely chop the remaining one-third of peaches and combine with puree. Add additional honey until you can taste it. Note: Make the pops a tad sweeter than you think they should be. They lose a little sweetness after freezing.

Pour the mixture into your ice pop molds (or Dixie Cups!), leaving a little bit of clearance at the top for the expansion that occurs when liquids freeze. Insert sticks and freeze until solid, 4–5 hours.

# PeteZaaz

766 CLASSON AVENUE, CROWN HEIGHTS
(718) 230-9229
PETEZAAZ.COM
OWNER: PETE ENTNER

Growing up in Marine Park, Pete Entner was raised on some pretty iconic slices. "L&B, all the way," he says, solemnly raising a fist. But when it came down to opening his own out-of-the-box pie shop on an undeveloped strip of Crown Heights, he wasn't content to play it safe with tomato sauce and mozzarella. Take the best-selling baked potato pie, which he tops with purple spuds, crème fraîche, cheddar, bacon, and green onion, and the coconut tofu pie, a Southeast Asian assortment of coconut milk béchamel, fried tofu, Thai basil, and bean sprouts. "My whole plan was to bring a gourmet style of food down to a level everyone can afford," Entner says, as he parks his bike by the take-out window of the tenement storefront and adjusts his baseball cap so it's angled sideways. "And what food is more fun to utilize in this type of economy right now than pizza?"

It turns out Entner has been having fun with food from the beginning, frequently whipping up meals as a kid for himself and his sister. "I always knew I wanted to be a chef. I started by putting parsley in Campbell's soup, and graduated from that," he grins. And although Entner is undeniably the captain of his motley Classon Avenue crew, everyone is invited along for the ride. The staff gathers together for regular brainstorming sessions, in order to come up with wacky new combos that toe the line between being crazy delicious (cold fried chicken), and just plain nuts (pickled blueberry). "I didn't think that one was going to be very good: creamy horseradish sauce, deep-fried eggs, and a pickled blueberry gusher," Entner laughs. "But people still come in and ask for it all the time."

# Coconut Tofu Pizza

(MAKES 1 PIE)

Wood-burning ovens may be all the rage, but Entner decided to stick with gas—meaning it's even easier to replicate his pies at home. "Order 2½-inch pizza stones, which retain heat up to 700°F," Entner suggests. "They'll make the bottom of your oven as hot as a wood-burning stove, if not hotter."

*For the tofu topping:*

1 bag shredded coconut
3 shallots, cut into rings and fried
1 cup cornstarch
2 egg whites
1 (16-ounce) pack extra-firm tofu, cubed
Salt
Vegetable oil

*For the sauce:*

⅓ pint picked Thai basil
¼ pint picked cilantro
¼ pint picked parsley
2 cans coconut milk
1 pinch ground chile flakes
2 cloves garlic
1 tablespoon onion powder
¼ pint chopped scallions
¼ cup melted butter
¼ cup flour
Salt to taste

*To finish:*

1 round fresh pizza dough, approx ½ pound
¼ pound bean sprouts
¼ pound Thai basil, chopped
¼ pound coarsely chopped peanuts
Juice of 1 lime
¼ pound fresh mozzarella, shredded
Olive oil

To make the topping: Spread coconut in a shallow layer on a sheet pan. Place in a low oven and let it dry out completely. Put the coconut and fried shallots in a food processor. Grind until almost powder. Combine the cornstarch and egg whites. It should have an Elmer's Glue consistency. Season tofu with salt. Dunk the tofu into the "glue" so it's completely covered. Roll the tofu in the coconut breading until fully covered and dry. Let sit on a full sheet tray until the glue has fully dried. Sear tofu in a lightly oiled pan until golden brown on all sides.

To make the sauce: Pick the herb leaves from their stems, and add all of the ingredients, except for the butter, flour, and salt to a pot. Bring to a simmer. Cook for at least 30 minutes. Add the coconut milk mixture to a blender and pulse. In a saucepan, add the butter and flour to make a roux, stirring constantly until a light golden brown. Add your milk to the roux, cook until slightly thickened, and add salt to taste.

To make the pizza: Heat an oven to 500°F. Once it comes to temperature, switch to broil. Stretch dough to ½-inch thickness on a lightly greased pan. Bake for 10–15 minutes, or until crust turns golden brown.

Mix together sprouts, Thai basil, peanuts, salt, olive oil, and lime juice, setting aside the rendered lime shell. Top crust with sauce, shredded mozzarella, sprout salad, fried tofu, salt, and a drizzle of olive oil. Rub the exposed edges of the crust with the rendered lime, and serve.

# PETIT OVEN

276 BAY RIDGE AVENUE, BAY RIDGE
(718) 833-3443
PETITOVEN.COM
CHEF/OWNER: KATARZYNA PLOSZAJ
OWNER: NICOLE GUARINO

Petit Oven in Bay Ridge is cozy, to say the least. A tight cluster of two- and four-top tables barely seats thirty, with minimal wiggle room. A refined menu of classic French dishes is brief—it needs to be, considering there's usually only one person working all the burners. That would be Chef/Owner Katarzyna "Kat" Ploszaj, whose shock of white-blonde hair is easily identifiable from the dining area as she navigates her (petite) kitchen—alternately shucking oysters, rolling fresh pasta, reducing beurre blanc, slow-baking salmon, searing free-range chicken, and dishing up wedges of her famous bread pudding with salted caramel. It's a game-changer for Bay Ridge's restaurant scene, which was a bit behind the eight ball on the "local/seasonal" trend when Petit Oven opened five and a half years ago. "I've lived in Bay Ridge for over fifteen years, so I knew, when I finally opened my own restaurant, I wanted it to be here," Ploszaj said. "I grew up on a farm in Poland, knowing

where my food came from; I remember my grandfather butchering a whole pig to make kielbasa," she continued. "And although no one was doing this kind of food at the time in Bay Ridge—local, seasonal, changing the menu every day, I trusted that people in this neighborhood cared about where their food was coming from too."

Despite the ever-evolving menu, a growing number of regulars lie in wait for particular dishes—placing calls to Ploszaj for a hint of when they might just reappear. "I have a very big pork belly following," laughs Ploszaj. "Especially our play on pork and beans—slow-braised pork belly brined for 48 hours, Asian-influenced bean cassoulet, and some nice, local sautéed kale." Not that you should revert to a can of Heinz if that pork belly is a Petit Oven no-show—this recipe is easy enough to make in your own little kitchen at home.

## PORK BELLY & BEANS

(SERVES 4)

*For the pork belly:*

3 pounds pork belly
1 cup sugar, plus extra for seasoning
1 cup salt, plus extra for seasoning
2 tablespoons whole peppercorns
Ground black pepper

*For the bean cassoulet:*

1 pound bag dried white beans (soak overnight in water)
1 carrot, chopped
1 small onion, chopped
2 celery ribs, chopped
1 (28-ounce) can of whole tomatoes
3 bay leaves
Salt and pepper

*For serving:*

1 stalk of celery, finely diced
1 shallot, finely diced
1 jalapeño, finely diced
1 teaspoon sesame oil
2 tablespoons soy sauce
1 teaspoon nam pla (fish sauce)

Score the fat side of the pork belly. Rub in the sugar, salt, and peppercorns, and refrigerate for 24 hours. Rinse the pork belly and pat dry. Season with a little salt, sugar, and ground black pepper. Put in a baking dish with ½ inch of water. Bake at 300°F for three hours, or until the meat pulls away easily with a fork. Add more water if necessary. Raise the temperature to 375°F and bake until the pork belly is a deep golden brown.

Place the beans, vegetables, tomatoes, and bay leaves in a large pot, and cover by two inches with cold water. Place over medium heat and bring to a boil. Reduce heat to low, cover, and simmer, stirring occasionally, until beans are tender, about 1 to 1½ hours. Do not add salt and pepper until the end. Just before serving, mix in the celery, shallot, jalapeño, sesame oil, soy sauce, and nam pla.

# Summer Chilled Corn Bisque with Grilled Curried Shrimp

### (SERVES 8)

Chef's Note: This recipe was inspired by one of the greatest chefs I've ever had the pleasure of working with, Christopher Lee.

*For the corn bisque:*

2 tablespoons vegetable oil

½ cup chopped onion

2 cloves garlic, sliced thin

4 cups water or chicken stock

2 cups fresh plus 1 cup frozen corn kernels

1 bay leaf

5 sprigs fresh thyme

1 whole star anise

1 teaspoon salt

½ cup heavy cream

*For the shrimp:*

1 pound medium shrimp, peeled and deveined

¼ cup buttermilk

2 garlic cloves, smashed

Olive oil

Salt and pepper

*For the shrimp vinaigrette:*

Zest and juice from 1 lemon

5 sprigs parsley, chopped

5 sprigs cilantro, chopped

2 tablespoons mayonnaise

1 teaspoon fresh curry powder

1 teaspoon fish sauce (found at Asian markets)

For the corn bisque, heat oil in large saucepan on medium-high heat. Add onion and garlic; cook and stir for 2 minutes or until translucent. Add water, corn, bay leaf, thyme, star anise, and salt. Bring to boil. Reduce heat to low and simmer for 25 minutes. Add heavy cream and simmer 5 minutes. Remove bay leaf, thyme, and star anise. Puree soup in batches in a blender, with center part of cover removed to let steam escape, on high speed until smooth. Refrigerate until ready to serve.

Marinate shrimp in buttermilk and garlic for 10 minutes. Remove and pat dry on paper towels. Let the shrimp stand at room temperature for about 10 minutes. Preheat a grill until it's smoking. Baste shrimp with olive oil, salt, and pepper. Grill for 2 minutes on each side until pink.

Whisk together all of the ingredients in the vinaigrette and add shrimp. Chill.

To serve, place 3 or 4 shrimp in a bowl, and ladle the chilled corn bisque around them.

Enjoy with a Meursault or an oaky Chardonnay!

# PORK SLOPE

247 5TH AVENUE, PARK SLOPE
(718) 768-7675
PORKSLOPEBROOKLYN.COM
OWNERS: CHEF DALE TALDE, JOHN BUSH, AND DAVID MASSONI

With a name like Pork Slope, it's almost a transgression to order anything from the menu that didn't formerly have a snout. After all, items like pulled pork sandwiches, St. Louis ribs, BLTs, and the house special Porky Melt (sausage patties, caramelized onions, and melted cheese on marble rye) serve as edible mission statements for the swine-adulating roadhouse—perfect for pairing with beer and pool under the glassy-eyed gaze of the two taxidermied boar heads on the wall. "To be honest with you, it's so fun. To me, the food is fun. We will never open a restaurant that's stuffy and over-conceptualized, where people have to tell you how and what to eat," says chef and co-owner Dale Talde.

The come-as-you-are bar also officially solidifies Talde and his partners' steadfast allegiance to Park Slope, becoming the third local eatery they've opened in the last few years. "I loved Manhattan in my twenties, but in my late thirties I started realizing that it's a giant NYU dorm now," asserts co-owner John Bush. "Brooklyn reminds me of when I first moved to Manhattan. I know the people in the bodegas, I know the people from the stores, I wave at people that walk by all day. That's the community I want to be part of and serve my food and drinks to."

# THE PORKY MELT

(SERVES 6)

*For the bratwurst:*

1½ pounds extra-fatty pork shoulder, cut and trimmed

½ pound ground beef

2 tablespoons salt

½ teaspoon white pepper

½ teaspoon ground ginger

½ teaspoon ground nutmeg

5 tablespoons nonfat dry milk powder

1 cold whole egg, beaten

½ cup cream

¼ pound cheddar cheese, diced small

*For the sandwiches (per person):*

1 (6-ounce) bratwurst patty

1 slice cheddar cheese

2 pieces marble rye bread, buttered and toasted

1 slice yellow onion, grilled

Salt and pepper

Oil for grilling

Deli mustard to taste

To make the bratwurst: With a knife, cut fatty pork shoulder into medium dice and mix with ground beef. Season with dry spices and dry milk, and grind through a medium-die meat grinder. Or ask butcher to grind extra-fatty pork shoulder, then at home, mix ground pork shoulder and ground beef with all dry spices and dry milk by hand or with a stand mixer. Combine beaten egg and cream, and using a paddle attachment, mix into meats. Fold in cheddar cheese. By hand, portion into 6-ounce patties.

To make the sandwiches: In a cast-iron pan or griddle, cook patties on medium heat in 1–2 tablespoons of oil for 3–4 minutes. Flip over, and cook for another 3–4 minutes. When patties are almost done cooking (around 2½ minutes), add a slice of cheddar cheese (or shredded cheese) on top of each patty. Melt cheese by using a lid (or another pan) to cover. When cheese is completely melted and patties are cooked through, remove and put to the side.

Butter one side of each slice of bread and toast in cast-iron pan or griddle at medium heat until it turns golden brown on each side. Remove and set aside. Cut onions into ¼-inch thick round slices, grill on high heat with salt, pepper and oil, for about 3 minutes. Place in a bowl and wrap with plastic wrap—they will continue cooking. Spread deli mustard on non-buttered side of each slice of marble rye bread. Stack patty, add onion, and top with other slice of bread.

# PROSPECT

773 FULTON STREET, FORT GREENE
(718) 596-6826
PROSPECTBK.COM
CO-OWNER/EXECUTIVE CHEF: KYLE McCLELLAND
CHEF DE CUISINE: VINSON PETRILLO

Their food looks ready to be photographed, framed, and hung in an art gallery, and their spice rack contains tubs of soy lecithin and xanthan gum. But chefs Kyle McClelland and Vinson Petrillo insist that they're all about straightforward cooking. "We're both classically trained, and those techniques serve as the backbone of everything we do," assures McClelland.

"We broil and sauté, but we also *sous vide,*" adds Petrillo. "We use molecular gastronomy to stabilize a cream puree or thicken a sauce properly. But when it comes down to it, we're just cooking food. All we're doing is taking ingredients and maximizing their potential." Certainly, one of the most appealing aspects of Prospect is being able to perch at a marble counter overlooking the kitchen, watching the two chefs work in tandem like a well-oiled machine, hunched over with tweezers, rolling carrots in hay ash, and constructing dishes as breathtaking to look at they are intensely enjoyable to eat.

Take the pan-roasted turbot, perched atop a vibrantly green sauce of stinging nettle (which tastes like a cross between spinach and arugula), and strewn with a colorful array of edible blossoms and herbs (either found in farmers' markets or sourced online). Although when it comes to re-creating that perfectly seared fish at home, you might be surprised to learn the chef's secret weapon. "Pam spray is the most important thing," laughs Petrillo.

"Get a hot pan, do a little bit of Pam spray, put some extra oil in the pan, and just baste your fish with that oil; never flip it," advises McClelland. "You'll be good to go."

# Pan-Roasted Greenland Turbot
## with Stinging Nettle & Buttermilk Nage, Hon-Shimeji Mushrooms & Various Blossoms & Herbs

(SERVES 2)

*For the nage:*

1 cup picked and blanched nettle leaves
¼ cup blanched spinach leaves
¼ cup blanched arugula leaves
1 quart buttermilk
1 teaspoon xanthan gum (a gluten alternative that can be found in health food stores)
Salt to taste

*For the turbot:*

1 pound center-cut turbot, trimmed and cut into two 6-ounce portions
Salt and pepper
Pam spray
⅓ cup canola oil
2 cloves peeled and crushed garlic
2 branches of thyme
1 tablespoon butter

*For the garnish:*

3 tablespoons olive oil, plus extra for serving
½ cup white and brown hon-shimeji mushroom tops
Salt and pepper
1 cup picked nettle leaves
10 arugula blossoms, leaves separated
10 mixed viola leaves, separated
10 micro red-ribbon sorrel
1 Meyer lemon

To make the nage: Bring a large pot of salted water to a boil. Make an ice bath using a large bowl or container with ice and water to cool the blanched leaves as they come out of the boiling water. Stinging nettles have small cactus-like thorns all over the stems and leaves. Using gloves separate the leaves and discard the woody stems. Blanch the nettles for 30 seconds and cool in an ice bath. You want to yield 1 cup of blanched leaves. Blanch the spinach and arugula in batches to make sure the water continues to boil for 30 seconds, then cool in ice bath. Squeeze all the liquid out of the leaves, chop into small pieces, and place in the blender. Add the buttermilk and process on high speed until the mixture becomes bright green and smooth. Thicken the mixture with 1 teaspoon xanthan gum and process for 30 more seconds till the mixture coats the back of a spoon. Season and set aside.

To make the fish: Preheat oven to 450°F. Season the fish generously with salt and pepper, spray the skin with Pam spray. Heat a preferably ovenproof nonstick or heavy stainless sauté pan over high heat and add ⅓ cup canola or vegetable oil till it ripples and is very hot. Carefully add the turbot, skin-side down. Once the fish is in the pan, give it a slight press with the back of a fish spatula to allow the skin to crisp evenly. Baste the flesh side of fish with the oil in the pan and place in the oven for 5 minutes. When the fish comes out, add the garlic, thyme, and butter to the oil and baste the flesh side of the fish for one minute off the heat. Carefully remove the fish from the pan so the skin side is up.

To prepare the garnish: In a hot pan with 3 table-spoons olive oil, sauté the hon-shimeji mushroom tops. Once they begin to brown, season them with salt and pepper, and keep warm for plating. Sauté the nettle leaves the same way, season with salt and pepper, and keep warm for plating. Pour 4 ounces of the nage in the center of a small round plate. Carefully pick up and begin to rotate the plate so the liquid covers the entire plate. Arrange the blossoms on the plates along with the mushroom tops and place the sautéed nettles in the center. Place the fish over the nettles, squeeze the Meyer lemon over the turbot along with some nice olive oil, and serve.

# "Yogurt & Berries"
## Yogurt Panna Cotta with Assorted Berries, Basil Sorbet & Hibiscus Consommé
### (SERVES 4–6)

*For the panna cotta:*

3¼ cups sheep or goat milk

1¼ cups sugar

2½ vanilla beans, scraped

7 sheets bloomed gelatin

3⅓ cups sheep yogurt or Greek yogurt

*For the hibiscus consommé:*

2 cups apple juice

½ cup strawberry juice, or blended
organic fruit juice

1 cup dried hibiscus flowers

2 tablespoons sugar

*For the berries:*

6 strawberries, cut into quarters

10 blueberries, halved

8 raspberries

8 blackberries

2 stalks rhubarb, finely diced

10 small mint leaves

10 small basil leaves

*For the basil sorbet:*

1 quart water

¼ cup corn syrup

⅓ cup sugar

½ cup blanched basil

To make the panna cotta: Heat the milk, sugar, vanilla, and bloomed gelatin to 110°F. Strain the mixture into the yogurt and whisk till smooth. Set into molds or into the dish you will be serving the dessert in and chill for 4 hours.

To make the consommé: Blend the juices and sugar in a saucepan and heat to 180°F. Remove from heat and steep the hibiscus flowers in the juice for 1 hour, covered with plastic wrap or a lid. Strain the liquid slowly through two coffee filters, cool, and reserve.

To prepare the berries: Toss berries, rhubarb, mint, and basil in a bowl, and set aside.

To make the sorbet: Bring water, corn syrup, and sugar to a boil, cool, and blend at high speed with the basil. Put in standard ice cream machine or freeze completely, blend in food processor, freeze again, then blend one last time before serving.

To serve: Divide berries among 4–6 shallow bowls or plates. Divide panna cotta (2 or 3 per person). Top each serving with a small scoop of the sorbet, and pour over consommé until it just coats the bottom of the bowl.

# Purple Yam

1314 Cortelyou Road, Ditmas Park
(718) 940-8188
PURPLEYAMNYC.COM
Chef/Co-owner: Romy Dorotan
Co-owner: Amy Besa

The strong aroma of vinegar and chiles hits us as soon as we walk through the door of Purple Yam, an inventive Filipino restaurant located in sleepy Ditmas Park. We've arrived an hour or so before dinner service to meet with chef and co-owner Romy Dorotan, who runs the three-year-old restaurant with his wife, Amy Besa. After ten minutes or so of silence, Dorotan finally shuffles up from the basement and gives us a sideways glance. "You're writing about restaurants? What do you like about restaurants?" he says, by way of greeting. "And chefs. Who wants to read about chefs? Terrible people." But isn't he himself a chef and restaurant owner? "My cooking is restaurant food, bad restaurant food." He laughs. "We've been taught how to cook badly." Does that mean he went to culinary school? "Thank god I didn't go into school, otherwise I would've been really bad."

Dorotan disappears back into the kitchen and brings out a steaming crock of chicken adobo (a fragrant stew of meat marinated in vinegar and garlic, considered the unofficial national dish of the Philippines), disparaging it all the while. He sets it down and lopes over to begrudgingly pose for some pictures. And then he laughs again. Smiles, even.

He mugs for the camera. We taste his "terrible" chicken adobo. It's every bit as delicious as we remembered, rich with coconut milk, fall-off-the-bone tender, and augmented by fiery Thai chiles and half a head of caramelized garlic. We wipe our lips, thank him for his time, and ready ourselves to go. And like that, his veneer cracks entirely. "Are we done already? Don't you want any more pictures? Do you have any more questions? And would you like a root beer float?" he asks us in succession. We're shocked. We thought he was anxious to get us out of here. Dorotan breaks into a wide, mischievous grin. "Oh no," he exclaims. "That's just my shtick."

# CHICKEN ADOBO

## (SERVES 4)

Chef's Note: For most people in my generation, fried chicken was really dry chicken adobo with the chicken braised in the vinegar, garlic, salt, and/or soy sauce mixture and then deep fried.

2½–3 pounds chicken, cut into pieces

1½ cups sherry or rice vinegar

¼–⅓ cup soy sauce, depending on how dark and salty you want it

½ cup coconut milk

12 cloves of garlic, peeled

3 bay leaves

½ tablespoon whole black peppercorns

3 Thai chile peppers (optional)

Marinate chicken in all the ingredients for at least 2 hours. Arrange chicken in a stainless steel or enamel-coated pot. Pour marinade over the chicken and bring to a boil. Lower heat and simmer for about 20–25 minutes until tender. Remove chicken and reduce sauce to a heavy cream consistency. Return chicken to sauce and cook for another 5–10 minutes on medium heat. (Optional: chicken can be broiled or fried before returning to sauce.)

Notes: My preference is to salt the chicken while marinating (about 2 teaspoons for a chicken) and to reduce the amount of soy sauce. I usually put the soy sauce in for color and a little bit of flavor, but I prefer the taste of salt in adobo.

Using coconut milk is a regional practice common to areas where coconuts grow in abundance such as Southern Luzon (where Romy comes from). The coconut milk adds richness to the stew and makes the chicken meat creamy soft. The sauce thickens a bit and coats the chicken.

# RED GRAVY

151 ATLANTIC AVENUE, BROOKLYN HEIGHTS
(718) 855-0051
REDGRAVYNYC.COM
CHEF DE CUISINE: AYESHA NURDJAJA
OWNER: SAUL BOLTON

Ayesha Nurdjaja grew up in Gravesend, in a family that lived, ate, breathed, and slept Italian food. So it's especially surprising that, when you ask her about her most formative food memories, she's more likely to mention hummus, tabouli, and kibbe than pizza, pasta, or meatballs. "My grandmother lived in Cobble Hill, and she would take us on walks down Atlantic Avenue to try Middle Eastern food. It blew my mind," Nurdjaja remembers. "That's when I developed a passion for spices. It just goes to show that the food you grow up with and the food you end up loving can be wildly different."

Not that Nurdjaja was able to ignore the call of her native cuisine for too long. Her heart eventually led her right back to Italian, where she rose from dishwasher to sous chef at Lidia Bastianich's flagship Manhattan restaurant, Felidia, followed by stints at fine-dining establishments like Il Bordello and A Voce. But it wasn't until taking the chef de cuisine position at Brooklyn Heights spot Red Gravy (ironically nestled among Middle Eastern eateries on Atlantic Avenue) that Nurdjaja finally came full circle.

"My whole life, I thought the pinnacle of my career would be to work with Michelin-starred chefs in Manhattan," Nurdjaja admits. "But having the opportunity to come here and elevate Italian cuisine with someone who's as accomplished as Saul Bolton has been completely amazing."

"And besides," she laughs, "being so close to home is a whole lot nicer than being on 59th Street and Columbus Circle."

# Strozzapreti with Caramelized Cauliflower, Taggiasca Olive, Calabrian Chili & Anchovy

### (SERVES 4–6)

¼ cup extra-virgin olive oil

2 ounces canned anchovy fillets, drained and finely chopped

¼ cup raisins or currants

3 garlic cloves, peeled and chopped

¼ cup taggiasca olives, or any black olives

1 cup chicken stock, hot

2 tablespoons butter

½ teaspoon chili flakes

2 large heads of cauliflower, cut into small florets

1 pound strozzapreti, or any pasta you prefer

⅓ cup freshly chopped Italian parsley

½ cup grated pecorino cheese

½ lemon, juiced

¼ teaspoon kosher salt, plus more for the pasta water

Heat the olive oil in a large pan over medium heat and add anchovies. Let anchovies caramelize for 2 minutes and add raisins, garlic, and olives. Let ingredients cook slowly, stirring, and after garlic is toasted add chicken stock.

Bring to a boil, then reduce to a simmer, and add butter to amalgamate the sauce. Add chili flakes and remove from the heat; return to a simmer before you add the strozzapreti.

Meanwhile, start cooking the cauliflower and strozzapreti. With a large pot of salted water at a rolling boil, drop in the cauliflower florets and cook them for about 3 minutes, until barely tender. Drop in the strozzapreti, stir, and return the water quickly to a boil. Cook another 4–5 minutes, until the cauliflower is fully tender and the pasta is al dente (Note: Cooking times may vary depending on the kind of pasta you use.) Quickly drain them and add the pasta and florets into the simmering pan.

Turn off the heat, toss in the parsley, pecorino, lemon juice, ¼ teaspoon salt, and a healthy drizzle of olive oil, and serve.

# RED HOOK LOBSTER POUND

284 VAN BRUNT STREET, RED HOOK
(718) 858-7650
REDHOOKLOBSTER.COM
OWNERS: SUSAN POVICH AND RALPH GORHAM

If there were a checklist for the types of food businesses it's possible to have in Brooklyn, then Red Hook Lobster Pound would have all the boxes ticked off.

They have a tiny takeout spot in Red Hook for ordering lobster rolls on the go, and a larger seating area right next door. They have a convoy of trucks (called Big Red) that regularly traverse the city and never miss events like the Food Truck Rally at Grand Army Plaza. And they were among the first to become regulars at Brooklyn Flea and Smorgasburg, although the novelty certainly hasn't worn off . . . lobster lovers have lined up in droves since the day they opened.

"It's pretty amazing, right? We've been enormously, immediately successful," confirms owner Susan Povich. "Before us, there hadn't been a lobster roll under $28 in NYC, outside of a traditional restaurant. It was the very beginning of the broader—I hate to use the word—artisanal food movement in Brooklyn, the beginning of what is now a borough blanketed with small food industries. And Red Hook was always in the crosshairs of publicity. People never quite knew what to make out of it. It had been an area that had been up and down, up and down."

"So I just feel like we had a great idea at the right place, at the right time," she continues. "My husband and I really believe we've created an institution that will always be here, but I don't need to be the Panera of lobster rolls."

So Povich may not have her sights set on a nationwide franchise. But it's certainly a testament to her considerable business acumen (along with the unimpeachable quality of her product) that Red Hook Lobster Pound has been able to bounce back as quickly as it has, considering how much was lost during

Hurricane Sandy. "Three vehicles and $50,000 in lobsters. I had six feet of water in seven thousand square feet and had to take my building down to the studs. I had to buy all new equipment and hire all new people. It was devastating," admits Povich. "But we were able to do what needed to get done, and come back in a bigger, better way."

## LOBSTER MAC & CHEESE

(SERVES 8–10)

*For quick lobster stock:*

2 leeks
3 sprigs thyme
2 teaspoons sea salt
1 teaspoon Old Bay seasoning
1 cup white wine
5 (1½-pound) lobsters

*For the cheese sauce:*

6 tablespoons butter, plus 2 tablespoons for later
⅓ cup flour
4 cups whole milk
1¼ cup reserved reduced lobster stock (above)
1 (14-ounce) package of elbow macaroni or gobetti
6 ounces grated gruyère
3 ounces grated mild cheddar
10 ounces grated Asiago
8 ounces mascarpone
½ pinch grated nutmeg
Salt and pepper
1½ cups panko bread crumbs
2 tablespoons lemon zest
1 tablespoon fresh thyme, chopped

In a large pot bring 4 inches of water to a rolling boil. Add all stock ingredients above except for the lobsters. Boil for 2–3 minutes. Add the 5 lobsters, cover, and keep at a rolling boil for 10 minutes. Remove the lobsters and let them rest—drain in a container that can catch their juices. (You can crack the lobsters now if you want to encourage more juice to be released.)

Add their juices to the broth. Then strain the broth through a fine-mesh sieve or cheesecloth and return to the pot. Reduce until there are about 6 cups of liquid.

Preheat the oven to 350°F. Melt butter, sieve in flour, and cook on low heat for 1 minute. Heat milk and stock, add it slowly to the butter and flour, then cook over low heat for 10 minutes, stirring until it's thick. Meanwhile, boil pasta in remaining stock (add a bit of water if necessary) for 3 minutes or until half cooked. When the sauce is thick enough to coat a spoon, add the grated gruyère, cheddar, Asiago, mascarpone, and nutmeg. Add salt and pepper to taste. Let rest.

Meanwhile, pick the meat from the lobsters (tail, claw, knuckle, bodies if you are so inclined), rinse off the tomalley. Clean and chop the tails in ¾-inch pieces. Do not chop the claws. Drain the pasta, mix in cheese sauce and lobster, and check the seasoning. Spray a 9 x 14-inch gratin

pan (I use whatever pan fills nicely to the top) with Pam, and pour in pasta mixture. Set aside.

Melt two tablespoons of butter in a pan. Add panko crumbs, lemon zest, and chopped thyme and cook for a few minutes on medium heat while stirring to bring out flavor. Spread the mixture evenly over the mac and cheese. Bake at 350°F for 40 minutes. Let cool a few minutes and serve.

Ok, we'll be honest. Brooklyn can't really lay claim to the rise of gourmet food trucks. But we do have a pretty impressive fleet. It all started in 1974, when independent vendors hailing from all over Latin America began gathering at the Red Hook Ballfields, selling traditional fare like sopes, arepas, huaraches, and horchatas to expats who would gather to play soccer on the weekend. It took a while (read: a couple of decades) for the rest of the borough's residents to catch on, but catch on they did. The Red Hook Ballfields became a seriously hot dining destination, with long lines snaking in front of the most popular trucks, like Country Boys (country boysfood.weebly.com), and Solber Pupusas (@solberpupusas). This eventually gave rise to another coalition of all-mobile eateries: the Food Truck Rally at Grand Army Plaza. Area favorites like COOLHAUS (@CoolhausNY), Morris Grilled Cheese (@morristruck), The Treats Truck (@TheTreatsTruck), Van Leeuwen (@VLAIC), and of course, the Red Hook Lobster Pound (@redhooklobster) currently assemble every other Sunday to feed the warm-weather revelers who flock to Prospect Park. Not that you need to make a weekend pilgrimage to Park Slope just to flag them down. Each truck maintains a regular route throughout the borough . . . just follow them on Twitter if you have a sudden craving for melted fontina and jerk chicken sandwiches, kimchee-studded tacos, and toasted rolls piled high with lobster meat. Brooklyn food trucks: They're not just for Good Humor ice cream and dirty-water dogs anymore!

# Robicelli's

ROBICELLIS.COM

OWNERS: ALLISON AND MATT ROBICELLI

What began as a friendly husband vs. wife competition in order to promote their specialty foods store in Bay Ridge (whose cupcake is better: Allison's famous classic carrot or Matt's chocolate peanut butter with gray salt?) has quickly given way to a flourishing cottage industry. "Within the first week of making cupcakes, we couldn't keep up with demand," remembers Allison. "We ended up operating a gourmet shop *and* a bakery, in a space that hadn't been built to be one. Matt was running the business all day, and then I'd go in and bake all night. It was an atrocious lifestyle."

They ended up shuttering the store in 2009 in order to concentrate exclusively on wholesaling cupcakes, and have since garnered a loyal following at places like Brooklyn Standard, Gourmet Guild, Blue Apron Foods, and the Red Hook Lobster Pound. They tend to rotate their flavors every three days, so you never know what you're going to get . . . although rest assured it won't be anything nearly as pedestrian as chocolate, strawberry, vanilla, or red velvet.

"We both grew up in Brooklyn, surrounded by the various ethnic cuisines of our friends," says Allison. "Within twenty blocks of our house there are markets specializing in Italian, Middle Eastern, Nordic, Greek, Chinese, Polish, Mexican, and Russian goods. It's very hard not to come up with lots of new ideas when you've always understood the scope of food is international and seemingly infinite."

That borough-centric inspiration is found in flavors like the Egg Cream, a Fox's U-Bet chocolate syrup–based cake, the Romeo y Juliet, a guava cake with cream cheese buttercream, the Odessa, featuring sour cream buttercream and sugared sour cherries, and The Breucklen, an apple cake with cinnamon caramel buttercream and *stroopwafel* pieces.

And now, all these years later, the Robicellis are looking to funnel their boundless creativity and energy into yet another Brooklyn store . . . exclusively a bakery this time. So has it become any easier to deal with the stress—financial, physical, emotional, and otherwise—the second time around?

"The truth is, yes, this business is our *entire lives*," admits Allison. "And for a while we thought that was incredibly unhealthy. But we've begun to realize that most people have hobbies because they hate their jobs. We love our jobs, so we never really become too wistful for things like painting or skiing."

# RISKREME WITH CRUSHED RASPBERRIES & ALMOND

### (SERVES 4–6)

Chef's Note: Pudding is actually my favorite dessert, and nothing else comes close to this recipe from my grandmother, who emigrated from Norway during WWII. She always made it during Christmastime, so we offer a Riskreme cupcake over the holidays too. Our boys assist us with making them, and since they're our kids, it's technically not child labor.

1 vanilla bean
1 quart whole milk
½ cup medium-grain rice, unrinsed
1 teaspoon salt
½ cup sugar
1 tablespoon butter
1 egg
2½ cups heavy cream, divided
1 pint raspberries
2 tablespoons sugar

*For the almonds:*

1 tablespoon butter
¾ cup slivered almonds
½ teaspoon salt
1 teaspoon sugar

Split vanilla bean with a sharp knife and scrape out seeds. Combine milk, rice, salt, sugar, vanilla bean and seeds, and butter in a heavy-bottom saucepan, stir well, and place over high heat until it just comes to a boil.

Immediately reduce heat to medium-low and simmer, uncovered and stirring frequently, until rice is very tender, about 40 minutes. Note: The exact time will depend on what kind of stove you have, but it does take quite a while.

Remove pan from heat and remove vanilla bean. In a large bowl, whisk egg with ½ cup heavy cream. Add a spoonful of the hot rice mixture to the egg mix and mix well to temper, then add the remainder of the mixture and stir well to combine.

Place bowl in refrigerator to cool and set completely—approximately 1 hour. While the riskreme base rests, prepare the raspberries and almonds.

For the raspberries: Place the raspberries in a bowl with the sugar, and mash with the back of a fork until berries begin to give up their juices. Set aside.

For almonds: Melt the butter in a skillet over medium-high heat until foamy. Add almonds and reduce heat to medium low. Stir until almonds become fragrant and just begin to brown. Quickly add salt and sugar and cook for an additional 20 seconds, then remove from heat and set aside to cool.

To serve: Remove riskreme base from refrigerator. Whip the remaining 2 cups of heavy cream to firm peaks. Fold into thick rice mixture. Serve with mashed raspberries and toasted almonds on top.

# RUCOLA

190 DEAN STREET, BOERUM HILL
(718) 576-3209
RUCOLABROOKLYN.COM
OWNERS: HENRY RICH AND JULIAN BRIZZI
CHEF: JOE PASQUALETTO

It can take a while for a new restaurant to begin offering brunch. And it can take even longer (if they attempt it at all) to start serving lunch. But three meals a day, seven days a week, right out of the gate? It seemed a risky move for the now two-year-old Rucola, quietly nestled among the historic brownstones in residential Boerum Hill.

But it's 11:30 p.m. on a relentlessly rainy Friday, and the restaurant is packed. In fact, it's remained steadily busy since opening at 8 a.m. that morning, and is likely to remain so well until dinner ends at midnight. "More than anything, we define ourselves as a neighborhood restaurant. It's our identity," says co-owner Henry Rich, who runs Rucola with cousin (and fellow Brooklyn native) Julian Brizzi. "We try to meet a neighborhood price point, and serve food that's healthy, but also good enough that you would want to eat it here two to three times a week."

Residents have been duly won over by Chef Joe Pasqualetto's rustic, Northern Italian dishes, which frequently showcase locally grown produce. For example, the tomatoes, eggplant, and peppers in a gloriously simple antipasto generally come from Feedback Farms, a micro green space right around the corner. "We have a more traditional protein-

to-vegetable ratio. We're not trying to cover things up in bone marrow or mask whatever flavors there are," Pasqualetto says. "We get a lot of great ingredients from a lot of nearby farms, and try not to manipulate them too much."

## THE FITZCARRALDO

(MAKES 1 DRINK)

Owner's Note: Since amaro is from Northern Italy, we use it a lot in our cocktail program. The somewhat bitter flavor also ties in nicely with the idea of rucola (or arugula) as our namesake.

1½ ounces rye whiskey
½ ounce Amaro Montenegro
3 dashes Peychaud's bitters
1 dash Angostura bitters
⅛ ounce demerara sugar syrup

Anisette, for rinsing glass
Lemon twist

Pour first 5 ingredients into a mixing glass over ice. Stir and serve neat in an anisette-rinsed rocks glass, garnished with a lemon twist.

# Potato & Salt Cod Soup with
# Oregano, Crouton & Soft-Cooked Egg

### (SERVES 12)

Chef's Note: This rustic soup really matches the ethos of our restaurant. It's simple, warm, and comforting, and although there's a little salt cod for flavor, it's definitely a vegetable-focused dish.

1 egg per each serving of soup

½ pound salt cod

3 tablespoons olive oil

1 medium fennel bulb, diced

1 small white onion. diced

1 medium carrot, diced

4 celery stalks, cleaned of leaves and diced

3 large russet potatoes, peeled and diced

1 tablespoon chile flakes

1 (28-ounce) can diced San Marzano tomatoes

Salt and pepper

Croutons (optional)

Fresh oregano

Boil eggs in water for 4 minutes, briefly shock in cold water, and immediately peel.

Soak salt cod in cold water overnight. Rinse thoroughly and dice. Add olive oil to stock pan, heat, and add next 6 ingredients. Sauté until onions are translucent, approximately 10 minutes. Add salt cod. Add water until vegetables are fully submerged. Add tomatoes. Cook at low simmer until all vegetables are tender and fully cooked, 30–45 minutes. Add salt and pepper to taste.

To serve: Pour hot soup into bowls, break soft-cooked egg over soup, and garnish with croutons and herbs.

# Saul Restaurant

200 Eastern Parkway, Prospect Heights/Crown Heights
(718) 638-5000
SAULRESTAURANT.COM
Head Chef/Owner: Saul Bolton
Chefs de Cuisine: Mike Tyler and Jesse Aghravi

Saul Bolton is certainly not resting on his laurels—or in the case of his eponymous Cobble Hill restaurant, Saul, his Michelin star.

Since splashing onto the Smith Street scene with his acclaimed fine-dining institution thirteen years ago, Brooklyn's busiest chef has opened the Vanderbilt, a casual gastropub in Prospect Heights, created an upscale concessions program for the Williamsburg movie house Nitehawk Cinemas, reimagined red sauce at Red Gravy, an Italian-American trattoria in Brooklyn Heights, and added a Caribbean accent to the overhauled menu at Botanica, the Red Hook cocktail and tapas bar. Oh, and did we mention that he owns an artisanal sausage company, Brooklyn Bangers, that not only keeps his restaurants in quality charcuterie, but is a regular at the Brooklyn Flea, and a featured vendor at the Barclay's Center as well?

"Maybe it's my desire to be liked by everybody," Bolton admits, "but being able to appeal to different kinds of people and different demographics in different neighborhoods really excites me."

He certainly seems to have the Midas touch. Especially when you consider that Smith Street, now a bustling food mecca, was practically a ghost town when Saul first opened all those years ago. "There were maybe two other restaurants here. Everyone advised me not to do it. But this neighborhood was kind of like a last resort," Bolton remembers. "We looked at all the obvious cool places, but we only had so much money. We lived half a block away, and they were offering this space at $1,100 a month rent."

If that prime location was procured by default, Saul's Michelin star—which the restaurant has received every year since 2005, the very first time stars were awarded outside of Europe—has been rightfully earned. But not because Saul is relentlessly white tablecloth and pretentious, with intimidating wine lists, overly fussy, precious fare, and prices to match. "It was a cool thing, getting that star. I'd dreamt about it forever and it had a huge effect on the restaurant," Bolton acknowledges. "But we've never tried to jump through hoops. It's not about the artwork on the walls, it's about the food on the plates."

That may change this fall, however, when the trailblazing Bolton abandons Smith Street for Eastern Parkway, becoming the new in-house restaurant for the Brooklyn Museum. Perhaps he'll end up with a Rothko or Degas after all.

# House-Smoked Sturgeon with Roasted Beets, Horseradish & Rye Crumbs

(SERVES 6)

24 slices of smoked sturgeon (you can use
　store-bought)
36 roasted, marinated baby beets
Rye crumbs
Horseradish yogurt
Dill sprigs

*For the roasted beets:*

36 baby beets, washed well
Olive oil
Kosher salt
Black pepper
6 sprigs fresh thyme
4 fresh bay leaves
3 shallots sliced
Red wine vinegar

*For the rye crumbs:*

10 slices rye bread
8 tablespoons unsalted butter
½ teaspoon each toasted caraway, cumin, coriander,
　fennel, and mustard seed, then finely ground
Salt

*For the horseradish yogurt:*

½ cup grated horseradish
⅔ cup whole-fat Greek yogurt
½ teaspoon grated lemon zest
Salt to taste
Lemon juice to taste

To make the beets: Preheat oven to 375°F. Toss baby beets with olive oil, salt, pepper, thyme sprigs, and bay leaves. Roast in covered pan until tender, about 45 minutes. While beets are still warm, carefully slip off their skins. Now season the beets with a little olive oil, a splash of vinegar, salt and pepper. Let marinate for at least 1 hour.

To make the rye crumbs: Take the rye bread and process in food processor until you have nice crumbs. In an 8-inch sauté pan, melt the butter over medium heat when the butter begins to foam. Add rye crumbs and toss. Moving and tossing until well toasted, add ground spices and season with salt. Strain the butter out of the crumbs, then pour the crumbs onto a few sheets of paper towel. Cool completely then seal in airtight container.

To make the horseradish yogurt: Combine the first three ingredients, then season with salt and lemon juice. Refrigerate until needed.

To serve: Generously smear each plate with horseradish yogurt. Arrange 6 beets on each plate. Sprinkle crumbs around each beet, like soil. Now arrange 3–4 slices of sturgeon on each plate. Garnish each plate with a few dill sprigs. Serve with a cold shot of vodka—just kidding!

# PETER LUGER: BROOKLYN'S OLDEST RESTAURANT

Stringent cash-only policy and notoriously surly service aside, Williamsburg's famed Peter Luger is also the recipient of a coveted Michelin star. And at 125 years old, the landmark steak house is officially set to take the "longest-running restaurant in Brooklyn" title from Gage and Tollner, which sadly shuttered back in 2004. Yes, many dismiss Luger's as an out-of-town tourist trap, or a spot to take the parents to, especially now that it's ringed by a multitude of notable eateries. But few can dispute the superiority of the glorious porterhouse steak, which arrives sizzling on a cutting board, ringed with char, marbled with fat, and pooled in its own mineral juices. Are there restaurants in the borough that offer a more inspired selection of sides and better-curated wine lists, that accept credit cards, and hire cheerier waitstaff? Certainly. But in the notoriously fickle restaurant industry, in a city where the dining scene is constantly evolving and ever-changing, making it past the centennial mark has to count for something.

# SCRATCHBread

1069 BEDFORD AVENUE, BEDFORD STUYVESANT
(718) 744-8231
SCRATCHBREAD.COM
OWNER: MATTHEW TILDEN

What does $3,000, a few plastic containers, some salt and flour, and a run-down pizza place in Bed Stuy get you? The greatest thing to happen to bread since, well, you know.

Although classically trained at the C.I.A., Matthew Tilden is essentially a self-taught baking guru. He began making bread while working at Chestnut in Carroll Gardens, in an attempt to offer customers a fully thought-out meal. So when he set out to start his own business, selling bread seemed like a no-brainer, although he didn't exactly have a lot of capital to do it. "I began with wholesale but mostly it was just hustling: make a couple of loaves of bread and find some places that wanted to buy them," Tilden said. "I had the opportunity to have a take-out window in my new space. So I started retailing on Wednesdays and there were fifty people lined up around the block each time."

The fuss certainly hasn't been over basic rounds of sourdough or standard loaves of Italian. Signature SCRATCHbread items include The Mutt (a hybrid of focaccia, whole wheat, and rye), Pizzabread (stuffed with house-made cheese curd, tiger shrimp, or spicy chicken meatballs), and even nonbaked goods like the Kale Caesar, a highly virtuous salad topped with soft-boiled eggs and a tofu-smoked almond dressing. "If you're going to pull off what I'm trying to pull off without any resources, you better be damn aware of what's working and what's not," Tilden says. "I also feel lucky that several people moved in around me, and the neighborhood has really just taken open arms with us."

"We have the best customers I've seen in any other place I've ever worked in," he continues. "They make our day because they're really excited to shop here. I've never seen any type of clientele that's literally just breathing so much life into something. It's really cool."

# Kale Caesar Salad

(SERVES 4)

**For the dressing:**

3 cloves garlic
1 (14-ounce) package tofu
6 tablespoons honey
3½ tablespoons sherry vinegar
½ tablespoon salt
½ cup olive oil
6 ounces smoked almonds
2¼ ounces salted capers
½ tablespoon toasted coriander seeds

**For the soft-boiled eggs:**

4 large eggs
2½ quarts water

**For the croutons:**

1 loaf stale bread
1 clove garlic, chopped
1 tablespoon rosemary
3 tablespoons olive oil
1 teaspoon each salt and pepper

**For the salad:**

1 large head Tuscan kale
4 cups croutons
4 soft-boiled eggs
1 avocado
Freshly ground black pepper
1 cup pecorino cheese

To make the dressing: In food processor, puree garlic. Add tofu. Whip until very smooth. Add honey, sherry vinegar, and salt, and blend. Slowly pour oil into mixture to make an emulsion (you don't want the ingredients to separate). Pulse in half of the almonds and all of the salted capers. Pulse in the rest of the almonds and all of the coriander. Taste for seasoning. If you want more tang, add more vinegar, or more salt, add salt. The texture is important, so don't overmix. You want the dressing to be coarse, not smooth.

To make the eggs: Boil water in 6-quart pot. Make ice bath with ice and water, and set aside, close to your pot. Set timer to 6 minutes 15 seconds, but do not turn on. Gently place eggs inside pot with slotted spoon, turn heat down to a rolling simmer, or about 210°F. Start timer when eggs go into the water. When time is up, remove eggs and immediately place in ice bath. Turn heat off of water. After 2 minutes, remove the eggs and peel them gently. When salad is ready, place eggs back in warm water for 1 minute to take the chill off.

To make the croutons: Cut/tear bread into 2-inch pieces. Toss all ingredients in bowl, place on baking sheet, and toast in a 350°F oven until light golden brown. I recommend toasting until crisp, with a little tender give.

To make the salad: Chop kale into bite-size pieces and place in large bowl. Add about 1 cup dressing and all croutons to bowl. Use your hands to massage dressing into greens. Coat evenly. Divide salad into 4 bowls, slice avocado inside shell with a spoon to desired thickness. Place slices on top of each salad. Place warmed egg on top of the salad, and finish salad with fresh black pepper and the option of grated pecorino. For sex appeal, just before serving, cut a small slice in the egg so warm yolk dribbles down the kale. Enjoy.

# Seersucker

329 Smith Street, Carroll Gardens
(718) 422-0444
seersuckerbrooklyn.com
Chef/Owner: Rob Newton
Owner: Kerry Diamond

Often referred to as Brooklyn's "Restaurant Row," there are few neighborhoods as chock full of top eateries as Smith Street in Carroll Gardens. And Rob Newton happens to own three of them.

After stints in some of the city's most prominent kitchens (like Le Cirque, Tabla, and Aquavit), Newton helped usher in the "Southern-fried" trend in Brooklyn when he opened his first restaurant, Seersucker, in 2010. Make that "Seasonal Southern," since the menu is just as influenced from the bounty of the Greenmarket across the street as it is by the cuisine of his Arkansas hometown. Think Cayuga spoon bread wontons with ramps, pan-roasted catfish with fiddlehead ferns, and bourbon-glazed pork belly with farm-fresh eggs.

"You know, people are going pork crazy right now, and Southerners have loved pork for centuries," Newton says of the restaurant's appeal. "And I think that when you talk about an original, market-driven cuisine, Southern food is that. People in Brooklyn are just crazy about markets now."

Add sustainably produced coffee to the list of current borough obsessions (which can be found at Newton's casual cafe, Smith Canteen), as well as elevated Southeast Asian cuisine (check out Nightingale 9, his Vietnamese street-food spot just down the street). And although Newton has found serious success and been undeniably on trend at all three ventures, he insists he's just fortunate enough to have been at the right place at the right time. "I've always done the kind of restaurant that I would want to go to, and it's always just kind of worked out," Newton shrugs. "I think the minute you start paying attention to trends, you're done."

# Bourbon Black Pepper–Glazed Pork Belly

(SERVES 6)

*For the brine:*

3 lemons, halved

12 bay leaves

1 head garlic, halved crosswise

½ bunch thyme

½ bunch parsley

1 cup kosher salt

½ cup honey

1 gallon water

*For the pork belly:*

5 pounds pork belly, skin removed

1 head garlic, halved crosswise

½ bunch thyme

5 bay leaves

Duck or pork fat

*For the bourbon black pepper glaze:*

2 cups brown sugar

⅓ cup white vinegar

⅓ cup bourbon

3 tablespoons black pepper

*For the slow cooked scrambled eggs:*

12 eggs

¼ cup heavy cream

To make the brine: Combine all ingredients in pot. Bring to boil for 1 minute. Cool down before adding meat to the brine. Brine pork belly for 24 hours or up to 3 days.

To make the pork belly: Preheat oven to 325°F. Remove belly from brine, rinse off and pat dry. Put belly in roasting pan, and add garlic, thyme, and bay leaves, and cover with fat. Cook in oven for 5–6 hours or until a knife goes through without any resistance. Allow to cool, at room temperature, in fat. When cool, remove the belly from fat and place on a sheet tray. Then place another sheet tray on top with weights, bricks, or large can of tomatoes to press for 24 hours in refrigerator.

To make the glaze: Heat sugar in pan until it caramelizes, then add the vinegar. Be careful when adding the vinegar; the sugar is going to bubble. Then add the bourbon and black pepper and reduce until it's syrupy.

To make the eggs: Beat eggs and cream together. Cook eggs over a double boiler, whisking constantly, for about 7 minutes until eggs are nice and fluffy.

To finish: Cut pressed pork belly into six ¾–1-inch-thick slabs, brush on the glaze, and grill until a nice char is achieved. Spoon some eggs on the plate and drizzle some of the glaze over the eggs. Plate the grilled belly and enjoy!

# SHELSKY'S SMOKED FISH

251 SMITH STREET, CARROLL GARDENS
(718) 855-8817
SHELSKYS.COM
OWNER: PETER SHELSKY

Stop your schlepping, Smith Street! Shelsky's Smoked Fish in Carroll Gardens is Brooklyn's answer to the gravlax-pushing, whitefish salad–peddling, sour pickle–purveying, Lower East Side businesses of yore. "I got tired of trekking to Russ and Daughters in Manhattan to get the kind food I grew up with," says owner Peter Shelsky. "Jewish delis and appetizing shops are such a huge part of New York's fabric, yet when the Jewish communities in Brooklyn got too religious, it sort of pushed out the appetizing shop."

"So many people walk in here and they're like, "Oh my god, that smell! It reminds me of Bubby and Zaidy's house," he continues. "And I think because of that, it's nostalgia food. People get nostalgic for the old-fashioned stuff."

That being said, the thirty-something owner is no Old Man Shelsky, muttering Yiddish expletives under his breath as he begrudgingly wraps up your quarter pound of Nova.

Shelsky has fleshed out his menu with a variety of tongue-in-cheek sandwiches, like the Brooklyn Transplant—fatty kippered salmon, cream cheese, and pickled herring salad on pumpernickel or rye—and the Dr. Goldstein Special; duck fat–laced chopped liver and apple horseradish sauce served between two schmaltz-fried potato latkes.

Shelsky also plays with unconventional flavors—curing his gravlax with Mexican achiote or Jamaican jerk spice—and sources his whitefish from Door County, Wisconsin, which he deems "the most insane whitefish you've ever had in your life." The leftover meat and bones are repurposed into an incredible chowder; a tasty play on the traditional New England favorite (sans the bacon, of course).

"It's great. It mixes the best of both worlds, you know; a New England–style chowder with smoky Jew foods," exclaims Shelsky. "What could be better than that?"

# Shelsky's Smoked Whitefish Chowder

(MAKES ABOUT 3½ QUARTS)

**For the whitefish stock:**

Bones and skin from 1 large whitefish
1 medium onion, roughly chopped
2 stalks celery
2 quarts cold water

**For the chowder:**

6 tablespoons unsalted butter
1 cup Spanish onion, small dice
⅓ cup all-purpose flour
6 cups smoked whitefish stock
1½ cups carrot, small dice
1½ cups celery root, small dice
1½ cups boiling potato, peeled and cut into small dice
2 cups half-and-half
Meat from 1 smoked whitefish (about 1 pound),
    in small pieces, picked through, no bones!
Salt and white pepper to taste

Combine stock ingredients in heavy-bottom pot. Bring to boil. Reduce heat to simmer. Simmer for 1½ hours, skimming occasionally. When done, remove from heat and strain out solids. In a dutch oven or heavy-bottom pot, melt butter over medium heat. Add onions and a 2-finger pinch of salt. Stirring regularly, sweat the onions until translucent. Add flour, stirring constantly, and cook for about 3 minutes. Add 6 cups smoked whitefish stock, stirring constantly, bring to a low boil, and simmer for 5 minutes. Add diced vegetables, and simmer for another 5 minutes, stirring occasionally to keep vegetables from sticking to the bottom of the pan. Add half-and-half, bring to a low boil, and simmer again for approximately 5 minutes. Add smoked whitefish pieces, return to low boil, simmer for another 5 minutes.

Taste the chowder, add salt and pepper to taste. The chowder probably isn't going to need much or any salt. The smoked fish adds saltiness to the chowder. Important: Be sure to gently stir the chowder from the bottom with a heat-proof spatula all through the cooking process, to avoid scorching; the fish and vegetables tend to stick to the bottom. For thinner chowder, add some additional fish stock or whole milk.

# Solber Pupusas

The Red Hook Ballfields at the corner of Bay and Clinton Streets, Red Hook

SOLBERPUPUSAS.COM

OWNERS: Rafael Soler and Reina Bermudez

"What makes our food special is that it's a fusion, just like our marriage," explains Rafael Soler from the window of his truck, as he deftly plucks hand-formed masa patties from the grill, and stuffs them with chicken, *chicharrón,* cheese, or *loroco,* a traditional, edible flower. "The *pupusas* represent Reina and El Salvador, and the chorizo we use, the plantains, the condiments—they are the flavors of my country, the Dominican Republic."

The fusion (and the marriage) is obviously working; Solber Pupusas has been one of the most sought-after trucks at the Red Hook ballfields for the last fourteen years. And in 2011, Soler and Bermudez even brought home the Vendy Cup—the top honor in NYC's premier street food showcase, The Vendy Awards—that has traditionally been a stronghold for Manhattan vendors. "It was the ultimate achievement and American dream for our business," murmurs Bermudez. "What we do feels so intimate, working with each other, making something together by hand," adds Soler. "To be acknowledged and honored for that is humbling."

The recognition has only boosted their popularity at places like the Brooklyn Flea and Smorgasburg, although Soler and Bermudez make a point of asserting their allegiance to the ballfields wherever they go. "We not only represent our business, but the entire Red Hook Food Vendors brand," says Soler. "That is why our truck's lettering promotes not just our business, but the entire Red Hook family as well."

"We cook as if we were cooking for our family, and our patrons, friends and fans are our family," Bermudez interjects. "After all, it's as much about hard work and love for what you do, as it is for the quality and taste of your food."

# Pupusas de Queso

(MAKES ABOUT 15 PUPUSAS)

### For the pupusas:

1 pound masa
½ teaspoon coarse salt
4 cups lukewarm water
3¾ cups shredded mozzarella cheese
1½ teaspoons vegetable oil

### For the curtido:

6 cups shredded cabbage
1 cup shredded carrots
1 cup white wine vinegar
1½ teaspoons black pepper
½ tablespoon dried oregano
Coarse salt
1–2 jalapeño chiles, thinly sliced (optional)

### For the salsa de tomate:

8 large tomatoes, cored and coarsely chopped
1 medium onion, coarsely chopped
1 medium green bell pepper, stemmed, seeds removed,
    and coarsely chopped
1 clove garlic, minced
½ teaspoon coarse salt
½ teaspoon freshly ground black pepper

To make the curtido: In a large container with airtight lid, mix all ingredients together along with ½ cup water until well combined. Cover and let stand for 2 days before using.

To make the salsa: In a large bowl, mix all ingredients together along with ½ cup water until well combined. Transfer to the jar of a blender; blend until pureed.

Transfer to a medium saucepan; bring to a boil over medium heat. Reduce heat to a simmer and cook for 10 minutes. Remove from heat and let cool. Serve warm or cold.

To make the pupusas: In a large bowl, mix together masa and salt. Add water, a little bit at a time, until a soft, pliable, nonsticky dough is formed. Using damp hands, form dough into 2½-inch balls. Flatten each ball into a 4-inch patty and place ¼ cup cheese in the center of each. Fold sides of patties over cheese to enclose and reshape into a ball. Flatten each ball into another 4-inch patty. Preheat a griddle and lightly coat with oil. Place patties on skillet and cook, turning once, until golden brown, about 4 minutes per side. Serve immediately with curtido and salsa.

# TALDE

369 7TH AVENUE, PARK SLOPE
(347) 916-0031
TALDEBROOKLYN.COM
OWNERS: CHEF DALE TALDE, JOHN BUSH, AND DAVID MASSONI

Between his three popular Park Slope restaurants, two high-profile stints on *Top Chef* (Season 4: Chicago and All-Stars), and omnipresence in a variety of local and food-related media, it can be easy to think you already know Dale Talde. He has an overriding love for Frank's RedHot and sriracha, and has handily taken the cheesy chinoiserie connotation out of Asian fusion food. He curses with abandon, and has confessed to attending anger management classes after his first *Top Chef* go-around. But there's also a lot more about Talde to uncover, if he stops moving long enough for you to ask.

Such as, if he could have, he would have become a basketball player, although he can also imagine being a serious dancer or in the army, due to his respect for militaristic precision and order. Or that he believes the job that really springboarded his culinary career was as a checkout boy at a grocery store, memorizing codes that allowed him to tell the difference between a standard plum and a sugarplum and a skirt steak from a sirloin.

"It's also where I started to see how ingredients come together, and in what cultures," Talde recalls. "You see a Mexican woman shopping for her family, stocking her basket with adobo and chorizo sofrito in a can, and you ask yourself, 'What is sofrito?' It forces you to actually look at that can and learn." Perhaps those early lessons are what

made him so great at breaking the rules later on—effortlessly combining various cultures on a plate, like pretzel pork and chive potstickers and fried oyster and bacon pad thai. "It's not too difficult to connect the dots on how I came up with that one," he grins. "I love pad thai, oysters, bacon, and crunchy things."

And after a confession that the cheeseburgers at Pork Slope are what he craves above all else, he's quick to tell you that Talde is actually the restaurant closest to his heart. "It's my namesake. It belongs to my family," he explains. "You see your parents work hard for your whole life and maybe get to a point where they can retire. And then they're kind enough and love you enough and have enough faith in you to support you financially."

"And I'm not a rich kid. My parents worked for it," he adds. "And I have to work that hard for them."

# CRISPY OYSTER AND BACON PAD THAI

### (SERVES 1)

*For the noodles:*

¼ cup vegetable or canola oil
4 oysters, dried and dusted in rice flour
1 egg
1 Thai chile, chopped
¼ cup red onion, sliced thin
1 bunch scallion greens, sliced
¼ pound bacon lardons, cooked crispy
16 ounces pad thai noodles, soaked
1 cup pad thai sauce (recipe follows)
¼ cup julienned carrots
¼ cup bean sprouts
2 tablespoons rough-chopped peanuts

*For the pad thai sauce:*

2 tablespoons vegetable or canola oil
1 tablespoon minced garlic
2 tablespoons minced shallots
1 teaspoon finely minced lemongrass
½ cup water
½ cup sherry vinegar
2 cups fish sauce
1 cup sugar
1 tablespoon sriracha
1 cup tamarind concentrate
1 tablespoon paprika
2 kaffir lime leaves

*For the garnish:*

Cilantro leaves
Basil leaves
Red cabbage, sliced into a chiffonade
Lime, cut into wedges

In hot oil, fry the oysters until very crispy. Reserve on a paper towel. Next, scramble the egg in a hot wok with a little bit of oil and add chile. Next add red onion, scallions, and bacon lardons and stir-fry. Add pad thai noodles and stir-fry until soft and wilted. Add pad thai sauce and toss. Next add carrots, bean sprouts, peanuts, cilantro, and basil. Remove from wok and top with red cabbage and additional cilantro, basil, peanuts and bean sprouts. Garnish with lime.

To make the pad thai sauce: Sweat garlic and shallots in oil until translucent. Add lemongrass and cook until aromatic. Add remaining ingredients and simmer for 20 minutes. Strain and discard the solids. Reserve the sauce.

Note: Extra sauce can be stored in an airtight container in the refrigerator for up to a week, and used as a dipping sauce or for stirfries.

# MARC SIMMONS: BROOKLYN'S OTHER TOP CHEF

In case you didn't know it, Dale Talde isn't the only *Top Chef* contestant in town. He's not even the only "Season 4, Chicago" *Top Chef* contestant in town. Meet Mark Simmons, the owner of Kiwiana on Union Street in Park Slope. The genial Kiwi is acquainting Brooklyn with nouvelle New Zealand fare (the nearby Hawker Bar and Sheep Station have us covered on updated Australian). Never thought you liked Marmite, the oft-maligned yeast paste? Simmons uses it as a delicious braising liquid for tender baby back ribs, served with squash puree and broccoli. Never heard of horopito? The ancient New Zealand herb adds a beautiful floral note to buttermilk fried chicken, accompanied by kale slaw, mashed potatoes and truffled honey. Are you in a protein rut, endlessly alternating beef, pork, and chicken? Take a chance on seldom-seen cuts like mutton, tucked into an abalone mushroom pie with smoked beet ketchup, or venison osso buco, with parsnip, white chocolate, and horseradish puree. Simmons may have been eliminated on the 8th episode of *Top Chef,* but one thing for sure, with food like this, we'd never tell him to pack his knives and go.

# Tanoreen

7523 Third Avenue, Bay Ridge
(718) 748-5600
TANOREEN.COM
Chef/Owner: Rawia Bishara

Even at 1 p.m. on a Wednesday, eyes ringed with liner and neck and wrists adorned with dramatic, hammered-gold cuffs, Rawia Bishara looks like the hostess at some highly glamorous dinner party. And for all intents and purposes, she is. Because a visit to the Bay Ridge restaurant Tanoreen is akin to stepping into Bishara's very own home. It's a chance to experience her warm hospitality and unique brand of cooking—which serves as a tribute both to her mother and to her rich Middle Eastern heritage. "My mom was a schoolteacher and she had five kids, but she cooked all the time. It was a beautiful tradition that brought the family together," Bishara says. "I opened Tanoreen to honor her, and I will never do enough."

What began as a love letter to Bishara's mother has actually worked to put Bay Ridge on the culinary map. After opening in 1998 in a tiny slice of a space on Third Avenue (known for years as Red Sauce Row), Tanoreen was one of the first non-Italian restaurants to garner serious attention outside of the immediate neighborhood. Bishara

eventually expanded into a much larger location just a few doors down, which still barely accommodates the crowds on weekends. "I've had to turn my husband away a number of times!" she admits, laughing.

That's why it's an even greater honor to be able to join Bishara on her real home turf—her kitchen—watching her gather ingredients to make lamb with *freekah* (pronounced free-kee), an ancient, roasted grain derived from wholesome green wheat. "Everyone is afraid about wheat, but this is so nutritious, so good for you," Bishara says as she runs the *freekah* though her manicured, purple-painted fingers and lets it drop gently back into the bowl. "Although it's been around for hundreds of years, I believe that it's about to become incredibly popular. So we're using it first."

"And now," Bishara says, as she ushers us out of her kitchen and back into the dining room to await her delicious dish, "I'm going to get *freekah*."

# Freekah with Lamb

(SERVES 8)

Chef's Note: I love to use *freekah* because I believe it's going to be the new, upcoming grain. It's incredibly healthy, high in protein, and picked while it's still green.

*For the fried nuts:*

¼ cup vegetable oil
½ cup slivered almonds, toasted
¼ cup pine nuts, toasted

*For the lamb:*

1 tablespoon allspice
1 tablespoon salt
1½ teaspoons fresh ground black pepper
⅓ teaspoon cinnamon
⅓ teaspoon nutmeg
3 pounds leg of lamb, cut into 1½-inch cubes
½ cup vegetable oil
5 whole cardamom seeds
3 bay leaves
3 whole cloves
1 onion cut in half

*For the freekah:*

⅔ cup olive oil
1 medium onion, diced
3–4 cloves garlic, chopped
1 tablespoon allspice
1 teaspoon fresh ground black pepper
⅓ teaspoon ground cardamom, optional
½ teaspoon cumin
¼ teaspoon nutmeg
3 cups freekah (can be found in Middle Eastern groceries, health food stores, or many well-stocked supermarkets)

To make the fried nuts: Heat ¼ cup vegetable oil over medium-high heat in a skillet large enough to hold ½ cup of the nuts in a single layer. Add the almonds first, reduce the heat to low, and cook, stirring frequently, for two minutes until the nuts begin to take on a golden brown color. Add the pine nuts and stir frequently for 1½ minutes more. Remove from the heat and, using a slotted spoon, transfer the nuts to a paper towel to drain and cool. Keep the oil to cook the freekah in later on.

To make the lamb: Combine the allspice, salt, pepper, cinnamon, and nutmeg in a small bowl. Place the lamb in a medium bowl and dump half of the spice mixture into it. Using your hands, rub the spice mixture into the lamb, coating all sides thoroughly. Set the remaining spice mixture aside. In a large pot, heat the oil over high heat until hot. Add the meat and sear on all sides, about 3 minutes. Add the cardamom seeds, bay leaves, cloves, onion, the remaining spices and 15 cups of water (enough to cover the ingredients and an additional 5 inches over). Bring to a boil and let boil for 5 minutes. Reduce the heat to medium-low and simmer, skimming the fat from the surface with a slotted spoon, for 40–60 minutes for lamb and 60–90 minutes for beef, or until the meat is fork tender. (Any remaining broth can be frozen and reused.)

To make the freekah: Heat the olive oil and the remaining oil from the nuts in a large pot over medium heat until hot but not smoking. Add the onions and sauté until softened and fragrant, 3–4 minutes. Add the garlic and sauté 1 minute more. Add the allspice, pepper, cardamom, cumin, and nutmeg and cook, stirring, until fragrant, about 30 seconds. Add the freekah and stir to thoroughly coat with the spice mixture, about 2 minutes. Add the seasoned lamb and 6 cups of the broth, raise the heat to high and bring to a boil. Reduce the heat to medium and simmer for 15 minutes or until the freekah absorbs all of the liquid. If the grains are not cooked enough to your liking, add broth by the ¼ cup and cook, covered, until it is absorbed. Spoon the freekah and lamb mixture onto a large platter, scatter the almonds and pine nuts over and serve with yogurt or shepherds salad.

# Thistle Hill Tavern

441 7th Avenue, Park Slope
(347) 599-1262
THISTLEHILLBROOKLYN.COM
Owners: Chef Dale Talde, John Bush, and David Massoni

David Massoni, John Bush, and Dale Talde are in the throes of a serious bromance.

In the last couple of years, the dream team (Massoni is in charge of all things front of house, top mixologist Bush works the bar, and Talde is executive chef) has launched two of the borough's most critically acclaimed, perennially packed eateries—the Asian-fusion restaurant Talde and the meat-loving roadhouse Pork Slope—and are given to frequent, unashamed declarations of love for each other on Twitter and Facebook. But recently, the threesome's personal and professional bond became absolute, with Talde stepping in as chef and part owner of Bush and Massoni's inaugural Park Slope institution, Thistle Hill Tavern. "We got tired of saying, "Well, we have this one thing, but then everything else we do together," Massoni explains. "Not to sound too overly corny, but the bromance didn't allow for there to be anything separate. Everything had to be unified."

Talde has certainly added some appealing signature items to the menu of casual, bistro favorites, like buffalo cauliflower and rice flour-battered fried chicken; although the group's rock-solid partnership remains their primary recipe for success. "I think one of the big things we realized early on is that this relationship is going to be longer than most

modern-day marriages," Massoni laughs. "And so it has to be treated like a marriage of compromise. It's about letting your friend win sometimes, even when you're dead-set on doing something a certain way, listening to each other, and constant communication."

# BUFFALO CAULIFLOWER

(SERVES 4)

Chef's Note: How do I make cauliflower taste the way I want it to taste? Oh, cover it in buffalo sauce and bleu cheese, and then it tastes like a chicken wing. That's how this recipe came about.

1 head of cauliflower
2 tablespoons plus 1 teaspoon canola oil
Salt and pepper to taste
1 cup Frank's RedHot Sauce
1 cup sriracha
8 ounces (2 sticks) butter, cubed
1 tablespoon crumbled blue cheese

Preheat oven to 375°F. Cut the end off the cauliflower and leave the rest whole. Coat the cauliflower in 2 tablespoons of canola oil and season with salt and pepper to taste. Place the cauliflower on a baking sheet and place in the oven at 375°F for about 30 minutes.

Once the whole cauliflower head is brown, take it out of the oven and let it rest. When the cauliflower has cooled down, cut the head into small florets and set aside.

In a saucepan, add Frank's RedHot Sauce and sriracha and bring to a boil.

Turn down the sauce to a simmer, then slowly whisk in the cubes of butter until everything is incorporated. Let the sauce cool.

Heat up a sauté pan on medium-high heat until hot, add a teaspoon of canola oil, then add the cauliflower and salt and pepper to taste. Sauté the cauliflower until warmed through, then add enough buffalo sauce to coat the cauliflower. Sauté for a minute until everything is hot. Place hot buffalo cauliflower onto plate and finish with blue cheese.

# Tom's Restaurant & Tom's Coney Island

782 Washington Avenue, Prospect Heights/Crown Heights
(718) 636-9738
1229 Boardwalk, Coney Island
(718) 942-4200
Owner: Jimmy Kokotas

Everyone has a "local" in Brooklyn, and we're not just talking about bars. It's practically a cultural imperative to select a diner in this borough—if only because it's a brief, inebriated stumble from your apartment. But Tom's Restaurant is a whole lot more than just a place to work off a serious hangover. Opened in 1936, the Prospect Heights institution has been overseen by three generations of family members (current owner, Jimmy Kokotas,

is the great-nephew of original owner, Tom) and has become home away from home for a countless number of New Yorkers.

"The restaurant has done a lot in a community that's been on a rollercoaster for the last forty years. It was German and Jewish when my uncles opened, with a lot more African Americans in the '60s," states Kokotas. "But even through the race riots, my uncle treated everybody with respect, black or white, tall or short, red or blue," he adds. "When Dr. King was assassinated, a lot of places in Prospect Heights were looted, and people actually lined up outside to make sure Tom's was not."

Even now that the neighborhood has become gentrified, Kokotas insists that 50 percent of his clientele remain loyal customers from back in the day. It's a devotion he hopes will extend to Tom's new outpost in Coney Island, one of the few additions to the recently overhauled boardwalk that residents didn't actively protest. "We didn't think it would be appropriate to try to duplicate the original Tom's, because Coney Island has its own rich history," Kokotas says. "It's more about the feel . . . people are coming in and feeling comfortable and at home."

"We're also trying to fill voids that existed in the neighborhood before," he continues. "Breakfast, for one. And having a sit-down restaurant is the other . . . a real, sit-down restaurant hasn't existed on the boardwalk in Coney Island for almost sixty years."

# TOM'S FAMOUS DANISH PANCAKES

### (MAKES 7–8 LARGE PANCAKES OR 14–16 SILVER DOLLAR PANCAKES)

**Owner's Note:** It's our most popular pancake. I tend to bring them to people on the house, just to try, and I'd say 95% of those people get them next time they come in.

1½ cups all-purpose flour

¼ cup sugar

1 tablespoon baking powder

½ teaspoon baking soda

½ teaspoon salt

2 eggs, lightly beaten

½ cup ricotta cheese

1 cup milk

2 tablespoons melted butter,
    plus a little extra for the griddle

2 teaspoons vanilla extract

1 tablespoon Parmesan cheese

Zest of 2 lemons

1 cup blueberries

Preheat a nonstick griddle. In a medium bowl combine the flour, sugar, baking powder, baking soda, and salt. In a large bowl whisk together the eggs, ricotta cheese, milk, melted butter, vanilla extract, Parmesan cheese, and lemon zest until smooth. Whisk the flour mixture into the wet ingredients until just combined (do not over mix). Brush the hot griddle with butter. For each pancake pour ¼ cup of batter on the griddle and top with a few blueberries. When bubbles appear around the edges and the pancakes start to fluff up flip and cook until both sides are golden brown. Repeat until no batter remains. Serve with butter and syrup.

# DINER LINGO

Despite the influx of fancy coffee bars and refined brunch spots, there's little as central to Brooklyn life as a diner. Where else can you get eggs all day, served with a side of attitude by wisecracking waitresses in hairnets? And except for a few modern updates on the classic greasy spoon (i.e., Diner, in Williamsburg, and Hope and Anchor, in Red Hook), most have been unwavering fixtures in their neighborhoods for a minimum of thirty years—think El Greco in Sheepshead Bay, Vegas Diner in Bath Beach, and Purity in Park Slope. And those are the spring chickens! Generations of Brooklynites have sipped cherry lime rickeys at the seventy-seven-year old Tom's in Prospect Heights, dug into mammoth slabs of cheesecake at eighty-four-year-old Junior's in downtown Brooklyn, and feasted on banana splits and burgers at Anapoli Ice Cream Parlor and Family Restaurant, which recently celebrated its 115th anniversary in Bay Ridge. Not only have these venerable institutions helped shape a culture, they've developed a distinctive vernacular all their own. Here are a few of our favorite diner terms!

**Adam and Eve on a Raft:** Two poached eggs on toast

**Balloon Juice:** Seltzer

**Black Cow:** Chocolate milk or soda with chocolate ice cream

**Coney Island:** A hot dog

**Coffee high:** Coffee with cream and no sugar

**Dog biscuit:** A cracker

**Fry two, let the sun shine:** Two eggs fried on one side

**Hot balls:** Matzoh ball soup

**In the alley:** Served as a side dish

**Jewish round:** A bagel

**Nervous pudding:** Jell-O

**Shingle with a shimmy and a shake:** Buttered toast with jam or jelly

# Traif

229 South 4th Street, Williamsburg
(347) 844-9578
TRAIFNY.COM
Chef/Owner: Jason Marcus

A Jewish chef cooking pork and shellfish on the South Side of Williamsburg, one of the largest Hasidic enclaves in the city, may seem like little more than a running gag. Especially when that chef calls his restaurant Traif: Yiddish for food that doesn't conform to the Jewish dietary laws. And yes, the cheeky irony may initially attract visitors to this corner of Brooklyn (the colorful space festooned with heart-studded piggies is also good for a laugh). But Jason Marcus's thoughtful brand of cooking guarantees their return, long after the joke has worn off. "At the beginning, I thought I should try to make sure everything on the menu had some form of traif. But the whole idea is that I'm not following any rules. So why would I set up all these rules about how the menu has to be?" Marcus ponders. "I'm not cooking these dishes to be rebellious, I'm cooking them because I love eating them."

That being said, the most talked about dish at Traif is undoubtedly the bacon doughnuts, and many other menu items joyfully flaunt pork in some form. "Even my grandmother, who had a kosher house, was all about going out to dinner and ordering BLTs. She'd say, I need bacon every now and then," grins Marcus. It's also easy to identify the traif in seafaring dishes like head-on prawns with black truffle and cognac, and soft shell crabs with pineapple sambal. So how does broccoli rabe with truffle toast and a fried egg fit into the concept of Traif? "There's sort of a healthy component to broccoli rabe, and yet, this is a very decadent dish. And that probably describes to a large to degree what I like about food," began Marcus. "I like that there's bitterness, sweetness, fattiness, and healthiness. There's crunchy and soft, elegant and homey. And this dish is a combination of all of the above. I guess you'd call it restaurant-worthy comfort food."

# Sautéed Broccoli Rabe, Portobello Mushrooms, Truffle Toast, Fried Egg & Parmigiano

(SERVES 6)

2 bunches broccoli rabe

4 large portobello mushrooms

1 cup extra-virgin olive oil

4 cups truffled béchamel (recipe below)

6 thick slices of brioche

6 whole eggs

Salt and pepper

½ cup vegetable stock

½ pound block aged Parmigiano Reggiano cheese

1 teaspoon truffle oil (can be purchased at gourmet markets and specialty food stores)

*For the truffled béchamel:*

4 tablespoons butter

¼ cup flour

3 cups milk

½ cup white wine

1 cups vegetable stock

1 teaspoon salt

½ teaspoon black pepper

¼ teaspoon nutmeg

2 tablespoons truffle oil

To make béchamel: Melt butter in saucepot. Whisk flour into melted butter. Add milk and bring to boil while whisking. Add wine and bring to boil while whisking. Add stock and bring to boil while whisking. Add other ingredients, whisk, and reserve sauce.

To prepare: Bring 2 quarts water to boil in stock pot and season with salt.

Preheat oven to 400°F. Blanch broccoli rabe until stalks are just tender, and spread on large cookie sheet to cool. To prepare mushrooms, remove stems and discard, brush mushrooms with clean towel and rub liberally with olive oil (about ¼ cup), salt, and pepper and place on cookie sheet. Bake mushrooms until tender, approximately 15–20 minutes. When they are cool enough to handle, slice mushrooms ¼-inch thick on a slight angle and reserve with rendered mushroom juice.

In a saucepot, combine béchamel and portobello mushroom slices and bring to simmer. Remove crusts of bread and drizzle each slice with 1 teaspoon olive oil and toast in oven until barely browned. Heat up 2–3 sauté pans with remaining olive oil and crack eggs into pans. Season eggs with salt and pepper and place immediately in oven to bake for about 2 minutes until whites have just set but the yolks are still bright yellow and just warm.

While eggs are cooking, sauté broccoli rabe in large sauté pans or 2 smaller pans with remaining olive oil and vegetable stock until all stock has evaporated and broccoli is warmed through.

To assemble: Divide broccoli evenly among six plates so broccoli lies flat. Place 1 piece of toast on each plate on top of broccoli. Place béchamel and portobello slices over each piece of toast. Place an egg over sauce and mushrooms. Drizzle 1 drop of truffle oil over each egg yolk and grate Parmigiano Reggiano cheese liberally over each egg (preferably with a microplane).

# THE VANDERBILT

570 VANDERBILT AVENUE, PROSPECT HEIGHTS
(718) 623-0570
THEVANDERBILTNYC.COM
CHEF: JIMMY CLARK

We have no idea how ramp-mania initially started. But there's no denying that in the last few years, the onset of spring has been officially marked by the appearance of the foraged wild leek on restaurant menus. "Yeah, it's all ramps, ramps, ramps. No one's like, holy cow, baby artichokes!" confirms Jimmy Clark, chef at The Vanderbilt in Prospect Heights. "By the end of winter, you start getting sick of potatoes and squash. And then, bam—here come the ramps. But they're gone in three to four weeks, so everyone tries to use them as much as possible."

Since house-made charcuterie forms the backbone of The Vanderbilt's menu, Clark has found a way to incorporate ramps (prepared three different ways!) into a best-selling seasonal sausage. "The dish came together two years ago when we did a Belgian beer–pairing dinner with Brooklyn Brewery. I made trippe, which is a mildly spiced, sweet pork sausage with cabbage ground into the meat," says Clark. "But the next week we got all these ramps in, and I thought they'd lend a wonderful, bright component to the dish. It's become a signature item at The Vanderbilt, and particularly popular in our tent at Brooklyn Flea." Since ramps have such a fleeting season, Clark recommends swapping in green onions and garlic for the better part of the year. But if you really want to make the most of this ramp-centric recipe, be sure to hit the farmers' market the second spring rolls around!

# RAMPWURST WITH SNAP PEA SLAW

## (SERVES 8–10)

Chef's Note: Keeping everything cold is the key to making sausage. Also, work the meat mixture really well with your hands. When you agitate it, the salt and water pulls the protein out of the meat, which becomes the glue that holds the sausage together after it's cooked.

*For the sausage:*

2 pounds fresh ramps

5 pounds ground pork shoulder

7 teaspoons kosher salt

½ teaspoon ground ginger

½ teaspoon ground nutmeg

1½ teaspoons ground black pepper

1½ teaspoons ground coriander

1½ tablespoons dry mustard powder

1 tablespoon freshly grated garlic

½ cup nonfat dry milk powder

1 cup crushed ice

1 pack of natural hog casings from your butcher shop

*For the slaw:*

2 cups shredded green cabbage

½ cup shredded red cabbage

1 cup fresh sugar snap peas, strings removed and sliced thinly on a bias

2 tablespoons kosher salt

1 cup mayonnaise

1 tablespoon spicy brown deli mustard

3 tablespoons chopped Italian parsley

1 cup sliced pickled ramp bulbs with ½ cup reserved pickling liquid

Salt and pepper, to taste

*For the pickled ramps:*

Reserved ramp bulbs from making the sausage

1½ cups water

1 cup rice wine vinegar

½ cups sugar

¼ cups kosher salt

3 black peppercorns

3 whole coriander seeds

1 clove garlic

Wash the ramps and separate the greens from the white bulbs (reserve the bulbs for the slaw). Bring a pot of salted water to a boil, plunge the ramp greens inside and stir for 10 seconds, then remove and chill quickly under cold running water. Squeeze as much water out of the greens as you can, then chop roughly and add them to the pork. Add the salt, spices, garlic, milk powder, and ice and mix by hand until the spices are well integrated and the ice is absorbed by the meat. The mixture should be firmly held together and sticky to the touch. Allow the sausage to rest in the refrigerator for 2–4 hours, then stuff into the casings and twist into 4-inch sausage links. From here you can grill, smoke, or poach the sausages depending on your taste.

In a large bowl toss the cabbage, snap peas, and salt together. Let sit for 20 minutes in a colander over your sink, this will draw out excess moisture from the cabbage. Return the cabbage and peas to the bowl, and dress with the mayonnaise mustard, parsley, the pickled ramps and their liquid. Season to taste with salt, pepper, and additional pickling liquid if desired.

To make the pickled ramps: Except for the ramps, bring all of the ingredients for the pickled ramps to a boil. Pour over the ramp bulbs, and refrigerate overnight. Remove the peppercorns, coriander, and garlic clove in the morning.

# VINEGAR HILL HOUSE

72 HUDSON AVENUE, VINEGAR HILL
(718) 522-1018
VINEGARHILLHOUSE.COM
CHEF: BRIAN LETH

Never heard of Vinegar Hill? Located along the East River waterfront between DUMBO and the Brooklyn Navy Yard, the five-block-square enclave has long been one of the borough's most under-the-radar neighborhoods. Until Vinegar Hill House opened there in 2008, that is. The restaurant garnered immediate attention for its seasonal-rustic menu and funky country farmhouse decor, drawing an endless stream of visitors more than willing to make the complicated commute (it's at least a 10-minute walk from the F-station) and patiently pound the cobblestone streets, waiting for a taste of their infamous Red Wattle Pork Chop and sizzling Cast Iron Chicken.

"Basically, we try to keep things simple and execute well," explains Chef Brian Leth of the restaurant's continued success. "People might initially come here because they've heard of those two dishes, but the menu is constantly changing and evolving. And it's nice to have people return just because they appreciate the way you cook."

Surprisingly enough, Leth considers one of his real signature dishes to be a simple Caesar Salad—uncomplicated yet whimsical—and topped with croutons bathed in every Jewish grandma's secret ingredient: chicken schmaltz. "I wanted to turn one of the oldest dishes into something interesting and delicious," said Leth. "Alright, I admit it . . . it was also conceived as a way to get a Caesar salad on the menu, so we can eat it in the kitchen as often as possible!"

# CAESAR SALAD WITH SCHMALTZ CROUTONS
## (SERVES 8)

1 egg yolk
5 cloves garlic, chopped
10 anchovies in salt, rinsed and filleted
2 tablespoons lemon juice
1 cup canola oil
2 tablespoons olive oil
Parmesan cheese, grated
½ cup schmaltz (rendered chicken fat)
Generous handful parsley, finely chopped
Stale crusty white bread, such as Sullivan
    Street pain de commune or similar
6 heads romaine lettuce
Black pepper

Add egg yolk in a blender with three cloves of chopped garlic, the anchovies, lemon juice, and a little water. Turn it on and let it run for 20 seconds. Start slowly emulsifying in the canola oil, then finish with the olive oil and a sprinkle of Parmesan.

Melt the schmaltz in a pan with the two remaining cloves of chopped garlic and the parsley. Add 1-inch cubes of crusty bread and gently fry until they are delicious, schmaltzy croutons.

Cut the romaine into ribbons, using only the light green pieces. Toss in a bowl with a generous amount of the dressing and croutons. Garnish with more grated Parmesan and black pepper.

# THE RISE OF SMORGASBURG

A tongue-in-cheek reference to the Scandinavian *smörgåsbord,* an extensive buffet that features a variety of hot and cold dishes, Smorgasburg more than lives up to its name. Brooklyn's mammoth, all-food flea market—held along the Williamsburg Waterfront on Saturday and DUMBO's Brooklyn Bridge Park on Sunday—features up to one hundred independent vendors, specializing in everything from deep-fried anchovies and Filipino spring rolls to dairy-free ice cream and artisanal pigs in a blanket.

Due to its tremendous popularity, a table at Smorgasburg has proved to be incredibly lucrative for vendors—bolstering online sales, garnering wholesale deals, and even paving the way for a few brick-and-mortar eateries (People's Pops and Mighty Quinn's Barbecue, to name just two). That means founders Jonathan Butler and Eric Demby have become super-selective as to who they let in. In fact, only thirty to forty new vendors out of over 350 applicants are invited to participate each year. Such a low acceptance rate—between 8.5 and 11.4 percent—actually rivals schools like Brown University, which accepts about 9.6 percent of applicants. Now that is one highly curated food festival!

# YUJI RAMEN

150 AINSLIE STREET, WILLIAMSBURG (OKONOMI)
(646) 262-1358
FACEBOOK.COM/YUJIRAMEN
OWNER: YUJI HARAGUCHI

With a food culture as firmly established and incomparably diverse as Brooklyn's, it's kind of hard to become the "first" at anything. And yet, Yuji Haraguchi was smart enough to ride the tide of a current craze (ramen) and bring a unique variant of noodles to the fore. That would be *mazemen,* a kind of brothless ramen that's only recently become popular in Tokyo. "In Japan, it takes people five seconds or less to eat the noodles out of a bowl of hot broth, but in America, it takes people 20 minutes on average," Haraguchi says. "That's why the *mazemen* style works so well here. It's almost like pasta . . . a great way to experience the flavor of the broth and the noodles at the same time without everything getting soggy."

Haraguchi has certainly used every opportunity available to expose the borough to the joys of *mazemen,* from a pop-up at Williamsburg's Kinfolk Studios to a highly successful stand at Smorgasburg. He was also one of the first vendors selected for a residency at Whole Foods cafe in Manhattan, where he tested out ideas for his first brick-and-mortar restaurant, Okonomi . . . which, thankfully, is located back in Brooklyn.

And while many of his dishes showcase fresh shellfish (Haraguchi was formerly a seafood supplier) he's finding more and more inspiration in the native flavors of NYC.

"I like to take ideas from diners or pizzerias or delis," Haraguchi says. "Like with my salmon and cheese *mazemen.* Except for, instead of bagels, we use ramen noodles!"

# SALMON & CHEESE MAZEMEN

### (SERVES 4)

Chef's Note: This original recipe is fast becoming a favorite at YUJI Ramen. You can use this recipe to do a surprisingly bold, warm bowl by plating with hot noodles or a refreshing summer starter by chilling the noodles in cold water before plating.

1 pound raw salmon fillet
1 pound Sun brand mazemen noodles

*For the salmon cure:*

½ cup sugar
¼ cup salt
3 tablespoons ground sansho pepper
1 lemon cut into halves, reserved separately

*For the cheese sauce:*

1 small wheel of Camembert
1 quart heavy cream

*For the sweet shoyu tare:*

½ cup soy sauce
1 tablespoon brown sugar

*For the garnish:*

1 bunch (about 10 leaves) of fresh shiso
1 tablespoon bonito flakes
½ cup kizami nori

One day ahead: In a mixing bowl or food processor, combine the sugar, salt, sansho pepper, and zest from half the lemon until evenly mixed. Remove the skin from the salmon fillet if it is still there. Portion the salmon into three similarly sized pieces. Toss the salmon gently in the rub mix to coat evenly. Place in a clean, airtight container and allow to cure overnight in the refrigerator.

To prepare cheese sauce: Cut the whole wheel of Camembert into roughly ½" cubes. Bring the heavy cream just to a simmer in a small pot. Add the Camembert, reduce the heat, and stir until the cheese is thoroughly melted. Note: The rind will not melt much, but should be allowed to soften. Puree the melted cheese mixture with an immersion blender or in a blender until smooth. The mixture should look like thick cream but not a thick sauce yet. Different brands of Camembert may yield slightly different textures. We use Hervé Mons Camembert. Pour the mixture into an airtight container and allow to cool in the fridge.

Day of serving: Mix soy sauce with brown sugar and reserve. Rinse the salmon thoroughly with room-temperature water and then pat dry. Cut into thin (⅛-inch) slices and reserve. Thicker portions of salmon may need to be cut in half horizontally so that the slices are about ½" wide. Roll fresh shiso into a loose bundle and cut across the leaf into ¼-inch strips. Reserve in a damp paper towel. Cook the mazemen noodles in a large pot of water at a high boil for 2 minutes, drain, and portion into 4 bowls.

Top each portion of noodles with 1 tablespoon of the chilled cream sauce and about 2 ounces of salmon. Drizzle 2 tablespoons of the sweetened soy sauce over each portion. Sprinkle bonito flakes on the salmon and cheese. Garnish with a small bunch of kizami nori and a pinch of the cut shiso leaf. Grate the zest of the remaining lemon half evenly over the portions. Serve.

# Index